Bonnie Bo

W9-DBU-050

Bonnie Bo

THE
ANNUAL
ENCYCLOPEDIA

T H E
ANNUAL
ENCYCLOPEDIA

John Kilmer

Crescent Books

NEW YORK

A FRIEDMAN GROUP BOOK

This 1989 edition published by Crescent Books
distributed by Crown Publishers, Inc.
225 Park Avenue South
New York, New York 10003

Copyright © 1989 by Michael Friedman Publishing Group, Inc.

All rights reserved. No part of this publication may be
reproduced, stored in a retrieval system, or transmitted, in any
form or by any means, electronic, photocopying, recording, or
otherwise, without the prior written permission of the publisher.

ISBN 0-517-67340-1

Library of Congress Cataloging-in-Publication Data

Kramer, Jack, 1927–
    The annual encyclopedia by Jack Kramer.
      p. cm.
    ISBN 0-517-67339-8
    1. Annuals (Plants)—Dictionaries.   2. Annuals (Plants)—Pictorial
works. I. Title.
    SB422.K73 1990   89-17262
    635.9'312—dc20   CIP

ANNUAL ENCYCLOPEDIA
was prepared and produced by
Michael Friedman Publishing Group, Inc.
15 West 26th Street
New York, New York 10010

Written by John Kilmer
Editor: Sharyn Rosart
Art Director: Robert W. Kosturko
Designer: David Shultz
Photography Editor: Christopher Bain
Production Manager: Karen L. Greenberg

Color separations by United South Sea Graphic Art Co. Ltd.
Printed and bound in Hong Kong by Leefung-Asco Printers Ltd.

h g f e d c b a

Dedication
To my old friend HVP Wilson

Acknowledgments
Thanks to the people at Van
Winden Garden Center for their cooperation

Part I
INTRODUCTION TO ANNUALS

© Daniel J. Rutkowski, 1990.

THE
ANNUAL
ENCYCLOPEDIA

CONTENTS

© Daniel J. Rutkowski, 1990.

Annuals are garden flowers with a difference: They provide instant color. Annuals bloom freely even with minimal care, and they keep their delightful colors for many, many months. Annuals can be grown in various climates; blooming times vary, from March to November, depending on your geographical location. To ensure that your plants succeed in your climate and geographical location, buy annuals from your local nurseries, which have many varieties ready for the ground.

An annual is a plant that completes its entire life cycle within a twelve-month period. Certain biennials and perennials also act as annuals. For instance, hollyhocks were once considered perennial plants, but now there are hybrid hollyhocks that bloom six months after seeding. Though these plants are not true annuals since they will come back the next year, they are best treated as annuals. True biennials need two years to complete their life cycle, but many will bloom the first year if seed is started early.

Annual gardens (opposite) *provide quick and instant color in
any color scheme imaginable. Sit and relax on the garden bench or
walk along a path and enjoy the beauty of mixed annuals.*

TODAY, MANY ANNUALS ARE AVAILABLE AS PRE-STARTED PLANTS AT NURSERIES (IN THE PROPER

SEASON). HOWEVER, MANY PEOPLE STILL PREFER TO START THEIR OWN PLANTS FROM SEED. I'LL

DISCUSS THE VARIOUS WAYS OF DOING THIS LATER IN THE BOOK.

THE NAMING OF ANNUALS AND OTHER VARIETIES OR CULTIVARS (THE WORDS ARE USED

INTERCHANGEABLY HERE) MAY LOOK CONFUSING, BUT IS ACTUALLY EASY TO UNDERSTAND. FOR

EXAMPLE, *ZINNIA ELEGANS*: *ZINNIA* IS THE PLANT'S GENUS, *ELEGANS* ITS SPECIES. CULTIVARS ARE

PLANTS THAT HAVE BEEN MADE INTO IMPROVED VERSIONS OF THE ORIGINAL SPECIES—TO EXCEL

IN FLOWER FORM OR COLOR OR FLORIFEROUSNESS—SUCH AS HYBRIDS. THE CULTIVARS ARE

DESIGNATED BY SINGLE QUOTATION MARKS, FOR EXAMPLE, 'BIG TOP' OR 'BORDER BEAUTY'.

Growing Annuals From Seed

GROWING PLANTS FROM SEED MAY SEEM UN-NECESSARY WITH PRE-STARTS AVAILABLE, BUT EVEN IF YOU GARDEN ON A MODERATE SCALE; GROWING FROM SEED WILL SAVE YOU MONEY—AND THERE IS IMMENSE SATISFACTION IN RAISING YOUR OWN. CHOICE IS STILL ANOTHER FACTOR: BY GROWING YOUR OWN PLANTS FROM SEED YOU HAVE A TREMENDOUS RANGE OF PLANTS TO CHOOSE FROM, MANY OF WHICH ARE SIMPLY NOT AVAILABLE AS PRE-STARTS AT NURSERIES.

Mail-order seed companies issue seed catalogs; some are veritable treasure houses of information. You'll have a great time selecting your annual seeds from the many catalogs available. You will be able to select spring and summer flowering annuals from catalogs mailed in the fall.

Plant seeds about six weeks before you want them to be moved to the garden. The seed packet tells you when to plant and how long it will take for seeds to grow. The planting date outside depends on your climate (hardiness zone) and the type of plant selected. You can start seeds in three different ways: 1) sow seeds directly into the ground 2) put seeds in peat pots or pellets (seed-starting kits) 3) plant seeds in cold frames or hotbeds.

Choose a variety of petunias (left) *for tubs and baskets from mail-order catalogs.*
Below: *In spring, garden centers and plant stores burst with color you can take home and plant.*

Below: *Lemon yellow marigolds, golden yellow zinmias, orange cosmos and pink wax begonias make a colorful summer border.*

Starting Seed

To PLANT SEEDS DIRECTLY IN THE GARDEN— AND THIS IS A SIMPLE METHOD—PREPARE THE SOIL SO THAT IT IS POROUS AND HAS GOOD NUTRIENTS. MAKE A FURROW IN THE GROUND WITH A HAND TROWEL. CUT THE CORNER OFF THE SEED PACKET AND SPACE THE SEEDS EVENLY BY LETTING THEM TRICKLE FROM THE PACKAGE. SOME SEEDS ARE SO MINUTE YOU CAN HARDLY SEE THEM, BUT DO THE BEST YOU CAN.

The usual rule in sowing seed is to sow twice as many seeds as you want plants, because only about sixty-five percent will germinate. Small seeds need little or no covering: larger seeds are planted two-to three-times, the diameter of the seed apart and covered with soil. After sowing the seeds, press them into the soil. Once the seed has germinated and grown two *true*

Zinnia angustifolia 'Classic' (left).
Below: *Label all seed-starting trays with variety name and sowing date to assist you in keeping good records.*

LEAVES, THIN OUT THE PLANTING BED AT THE SPACING SUGGESTED ON THE SEED PACKET. SNIP OFF UNWANTED PLANTS; DON'T PULL THEM UP, BECAUSE YOU MIGHT PULL UP THE NEXT SEEDLING (ROOTS INTERTWINE). TAKING AWAY SOME PLANTS GIVES OTHERS A BETTER CHANCE OF GROWING—MORE SPACE AND MORE NUTRIENTS. KEEP THE SEED BED MOIST AND SIT BACK AND WATCH YOUR GARDEN GROW.

Starting Seed Indoors

An easy way to start seed indoors is by using peat pots, which come in pellets or cubes and are available at nurseries. Once again, read the seed packet to find out if that particular seed requires darkness or light, the length of time to germination, and other pertinent information. Use a plastic tray to hold the peat containers. Moisten the pellets, and within a few minutes they will expand into small pots. Make sure these planters stay moist, place a few seeds in the small depressions at the top of each seed container, cover or do not

Below: *Summer border featuring scarlet sage, white petunias and pink nicotiana.*

COVER DEPENDING UPON THE DIRECTIONS ON THE SEED PACKET, AND PUT THE TRAY IN A LOCATION WHERE IT RECEIVES SOME LIGHT AND THE TEMPERATURE IS ABOUT 78°F (25°C) DAY AND NIGHT. KEEP THE POTS MOIST AND BE SURE THE SEEDS ARE GETTING GOOD LIGHT BUT NO DIRECT SUN. THIN OUT THE SEEDLINGS WITH SCISSORS, ALLOWING THE STRONGEST SEEDLING TO

REMAIN. WHEN THE SEEDLINGS ARE TWO INCHES (FIVE CENTIMETERS) TALL AND ROOTS ARE COMING OUT OF THE SIDES OF THE TINY POTS, IT IS TIME TO TRANSPLANT THE SEEDLINGS TO THE GARDEN.

DON'T JUST SET THE PLANTS INTO THE GROUND. THE SEEDLINGS HAVE BEEN GROWING IN A PROTECTED ENVIRONMENT SO THEY NEED A "HARDENING OFF" TIME. FOR ABOUT A WEEK, PUT THEM OUTSIDE FOR A FEW HOURS EVERY DAY IN SUBDUED LIGHT. LENGTHEN THE AMOUNT OF TIME EVERY FEW DAYS, AND IN A WEEK OR SO THEY WILL BE READY FOR DIRECT GROUND PLANTING. TAKE THE PEAT POT, DIG A HOLE FOR IT IN THE GROUND, AND SINK THE COMPLETE UNIT INTO THE HOLE. COVER WITH ONE-QUARTER INCH (SIX MILLIMETERS) OF SOIL AND MOISTEN. THE SEEDS ARE NOW READY TO GROW.

A well-developed plant (opposite) is ready to be moved into the garden. Below left: To make transplanting easier, seeds can be started in individual pots. Below right: Self-contained planting units called Jiffy 7s are flat pellets that expand into containers when moistened.

Cold Frame and Hotbed

THE COLD FRAME AND HOTBED ARE OLD-FASHIONED DEVICES FOR STARTING SEEDS. BOTH UNITS AFFORD PROTECTION AGAINST THE ELEMENTS FOR SEEDLINGS OUTDOORS. A COLD FRAME IS A BOTTOMLESS WOODEN BOX SUNK INTO THE GROUND WITH AN ADJUSTABLE COVER OF PLASTIC OR GLASS. THE COVER IS USUALLY RAISED A FEW HOURS EACH DAY TO ADMIT FRESH AIR.

Mealy cup sage and dusty miller (left) *can be started as seedlings in a cold frame if space is limited indoors. Seedlings of these mixed annuals* (below) *were started indoors and "hardened off" in a cold frame.*

A HOTBED IS A VARIATION OF THE COLD FRAME IN WHICH SOIL-HEATING CABLES ARE INSTALLED AT THE BOTTOM. THE SEED-STARTING PROCESS IS THE SAME AS IT IS FOR STARTING SEED IN PEAT POTS INDOORS, EXCEPT IN THIS CASE THE ENTIRE PROCESS IS DONE OUTDOORS. USE A GOOD SOIL BASE IN THE COLD FRAME OR HOTBED: INSERT A ONE-INCH LAYER OF GRAVEL FIRST, THEN ADD ABOUT SIX INCHES (FIFTEEN CENTIMETERS) OF SOIL. KEEP THE SOIL MOIST UNTIL THE SEEDLINGS ARE READY FOR GARDEN PLANTING.

Designing With Annuals

ANNUALS ARE INEXPENSIVE, EASY TO GROW, AND SUITABLE FOR ALMOST ANY LANDSCAPE DESIGN. IN NINETEENTH-CENTURY ENGLAND, ANNUALS WERE USED AS MASSIVE COLOR CARPETS TO CREATE THE MANY FAMOUS *PARTERRES*. WHETHER YOU ARE USING ANNUALS IN THE PERENNIAL GARDEN (TO SUPPLY COLOR UNTIL THE PERENNIALS BLOOM), IN THE VEGETABLE GARDEN, IN SHRUB LANDSCAPES, OR IN LAWNS TO CREATE DRAMA AS BORDERS OR DRIFTS, THESE VERSATILE PLANTS ARE WORTH THEIR WEIGHT IN GOLD.

Flower borders are important almost anywhere in the garden, heightening the drama of a fence or wall, creating character for walks and paths, and complementing lawns beautifully. Keep the border three to five feet (one to two meters) wide; if the border is any wider, it will be difficult to tend the rear plants without walking on those in front.

Flower beds provide color, bring great drama to a garden landscape, and are accessible from all sides. Actually, these accent areas are not really beds; they are drifts of color and are best when planted in wide arcs or ovals rather than in rectangles or other shapes. With careful planning, such drifts can make a garden extraordinary.

There has always been debate over formal gardens and informal gardens. The latter were in favor a decade ago, but now formal gardens are undergoing a renaissance. The garden to have is the one *you* want. Gardens are personal; some people like the formal symmetrical look, but others prefer plants more casually placed. However, there are certain dicta: If the topography is hilly and plants are mature specimens, such as trees, the garden may have to be informal, to adapt to the site. But if the garden is flat, you can choose either a formal or an informal style.

As mentioned, formal gardens are symmetrical; that is, the trees, pairs of shrubs, and other plants on one side mirror the plants on the other side. Some advantages of the formal garden are that you can grow handsome arrangements and do not need many plants. With the informal garden, you need more mass, so you have to use more plants with great expanses of color. The formal garden is green, accented with a few colors, whereas the informal garden is many colors accented with a

Below left: *The combination of yellow and golden marigolds is known as analagous color harmony.* Below right: *The combination of yellow and violet statice is known as complementary color harmony.*

FEW GREEN TREES OR SHRUBS.

TO HELP YOU USE ANNUALS BEST IN YOUR GARDEN DESIGN, CONSIDER THE FOLLOWING SUGGESTIONS:

- ♦ DECIDE WHETHER YOU WANT A FORMAL LOOK OR AN INFORMAL, COTTAGE LOOK.

- ♦ CONSIDER YOUR SPACE. DOES IT LIMIT YOU TO SMALL ANNUALS OR CAN YOU USE TALL PLANTS?

- ♦ WHEN CONSIDERING COLORS, REMEMBER THAT GRADATIONS OF COLOR WORK BEST, RATHER THAN ABRUPT CHANGES, FROM RED TO WHITE OR FROM BLUE TO YELLOW, FOR EXAMPLE.

- ♦ PLANT TALL-GROWING ANNUALS BEHIND LOW-GROWING ONES.

- ♦ STAIR-STEP YOUR ANNUALS TO CREATE DIMENSION.

- ♦ USE CONTRASTING COLORS AND FOLIAGE TEXTURES.

Growing Conditions

TODAY, SOME PEOPLE START ANNUALS FROM SEED IN PACKS AT NURSERIES. OTHER GARDENERS BUY PRE-STARTED PLANTS. GENERALLY, THE BEST PROCEDURE IS TO BUY AND PLANT THE ANNUALS WHEN THEY START APPEARING AT NURSERIES. THIS WILL GIVE YOU INSTANT COLOR IN THE GARDEN. ONCE YOU HAVE SELECTED YOUR PLANTS BY COLOR OR LIGHT CONDITIONS AND HAVE THEM HOME, PUT THEM IN THE GROUND RIGHT AWAY. IF YOU MUST KEEP PLANTS OUT OF THE GROUND FOR A DAY OR MORE UNTIL YOU HAVE THE TIME TO PLANT THEM, PUT THEM IN A SHADY PLACE AND WATER THEM WELL.

To grow lush, healthy, colorful flower gardens, you must start with an enriched soil (below). Opposite: Select healthy plants when you go shopping for annuals for the garden.

WHEN YOU REMOVE THE ANNUAL FROM ITS CONTAINER, BE GENTLE; PUSH OUT THE BOTTOM OF THE CONTAINER TO BRING OUT THE PLANT WITH THE GROWING MEDIUM AROUND THE ROOT BALL INTACT. SOIL AND WATER ARE THE LIFELINES OF YOUR ANNUALS, SO BE SURE THE CONDITION OF THE SOIL IS GOOD. WITH A SPADE OR A SHOVEL, WORK SOME ORGANIC MATTER INTO THE SOIL. NURSERIES SELL MANY DIFFERENT KINDS OF ORGANIC MATTER—FROM PACKAGES OF CHICKEN MANURE TO BAGS OF PEAT MOSS OR COMPOST. SOIL MUST BE POROUS. TO TEST THE SOIL, PICK UP A HANDFUL: IF IT CRUMBLES, IT WILL LET WATER AND AIR PASS THROUGH IT, WHICH IS WHAT PLANTS WANT. IF THE SOIL CLUMPS IN YOUR HAND, YOU NEED TO ADD ORGANIC MATTER TO BREAK UP THE SOIL. ADD ENOUGH ORGANIC MATTER SO THAT THE FINAL MIX OF SOIL IS ONE-THIRD ORGANIC MATTER. A TWO-INCH (FIVE-CENTIMETER) THICK LAYER OF ORGANIC MATTER WORKED INTO THE SOIL TO A DEPTH OF SIX INCHES (FIFTEEN CENTIMETERS) WILL PROVIDE A GOOD BASIC SOIL.

SOME GARDENERS WORRY A GREAT DEAL ABOUT THE ALKALINITY OR ACIDITY OF SOIL. MOST PLANTS PREFER SOIL WITH A pH OF 6.0 TO 7.5. IF THE SOIL IS FRIABLE (EASILY CRUMBLED) AND YOU HAVE ADDED ORGANIC MATTER, IT SHOULD BE ACCEPTABLE FOR YOUR ANNUALS (OR ANY PLANTS). YOU DO NOT NEED TO BUY EXPENSIVE SOIL-TESTING KITS OR ADD ANYTHING TO YOUR SOIL.

Feeding and Watering

GARDENERS HAVE BEEN LED TO BELIEVE THAT CONSTANT FEEDING IS NECESSARY TO PRODUCE FLOWERING PLANTS. ACTUALLY, MOST ANNUALS WILL GET ALONG FINE WITHOUT EXCESSIVE FEEDING. USING AN ALL-PURPOSE 5–10–10 PLANT FOOD THREE OR FOUR TIMES A YEAR IS SUFFICIENT. MORE IS NOT BETTER—LESS IS THE HALLMARK OF SUCCESS.

*Healthy, floriferous flowerbeds are a signal that
they are receiving the proper amount of fertilizer* (below).

THERE ARE LIQUID FERTILIZERS, DRY FERTIL-
IZERS, FOODS CONTAINING INSECTICIDES AND FOODS THAT LOOK LIKE GRANULES—ALL THESE
CHEMICALS COST MONEY. YOU ONLY NEED ONE TYPE OF FOOD: LIQUID FOOD MIXED WITH
WATER. FOLLOW THE DIRECTIONS ON THE BOTTLE. FORGET THE HASSLE OF USING SPECIFIC
FOODS FOR SPECIFIC PLANTS OR ANY OF THE OTHER FOOD ADVICE NURSERY PERSONNEL USUALLY
DISPENSE.

FEEDING IS NOT A VITAL ASPECT OF GROWING ANNUALS SUCCESSFULLY. WATERING, HOWEVER,

Below: *To keep your flowers in peak shape, apply water to the ground rather than watering overhead so the flowers are not damaged.*

IS CRUCIAL. ANNUALS NEED PLENTY OF WATER TO THRIVE. IF YOU WANT ABUNDANT FLOWERS, WATER FREQUENTLY AND DEEPLY. IF YOU USE A HOSE YOU WILL HAVE TO WATER FOR AT LEAST TWENTY MINUTES TO PENETRATE THE SOIL TO A DEPTH OF TWENTY-FOUR INCHES (SIXTY CENTIMETERS). SPRINKLERS ARE BETTER, BUT DRIP-WATERING SYSTEMS ARE BEST. THESE KITS (AVAILABLE AT HARDWARE STORES) TAKE SOME TIME TO SET UP, BUT DRIP SYSTEMS SAVE A GREAT DEAL OF WATER AND PUT THE WATER WHERE PLANTS CAN REALLY USE IT—AT THE ROOTS. DRIP-WATERING KITS ARE INEXPENSIVE AND PAY FOR THEMSELVES OVER A SHORT TIME.

Grooming

IT IS A GOOD IDEA TO PINCH OUT ANNUALS WHEN THEY ARE YOUNG TO ENCOURAGE GOOD BLOOM. THROW AWAY DEAD AND FADED FLOWERS; DO NOT JUST LET THEM LIE ON THE GROUND OR BACTERIAL DISEASES MAY START. STAKE TALL-GROWING ANNUALS (STAKES ARE SOLD AT NURSERIES). INSERT THE STAKES INTO THE GROUND NEXT TO THE PLANTS AND TIE THEM TO THE PLANTS WITH "TIE-EMS" OR STRING.

Putting Transplants Into the Garden

When you are ready to transplant your pre-started annuals into the conditioned soil, be sure to adhere to the following rules:

- Make sure pre-packed plants are watered, so the growing medium will hold together and you can plant the root ball, causing less shock to plants.

- Plant during the cooler part of the day, preferably on a day without excessive wind.

- Always handle plants gently; do not tug, pull, or rip apart those in flats.

- Dig the holes for the plants at least four to six inches (ten to fifteen centimeters) deep, and then firmly pack the soil around the plant crown. Put the plants deeper into the ground than they were in their containers.

- Water the plants thoroughly.

Final Words

Do not plant annuals in the garden until the climate is amenable and the soil properly conditioned. Wait until the spring season really arrives. If you are planting in shade, be sure to use shade-tolerant annuals because those that need sun just will not succeed. If your garden area is sunny, plant sun-loving varieties. Do not plant annuals too close to each other; give them space to grow. During the first few weeks the annuals may look sparse in your garden, but the plants will thrive with space. Annuals are fast growers, so do not cram too many plants into one area. Get rid of weeds as they appear or they will sap the nutrients from the soil, leaving your annuals to starve. Small weeds are easy to remove; large weeds can be difficult to remove unless you tear up the flower bed.

Part II
THE PLANTS

© Daniel J. Rutkowski, 1990.

Abelmoschus moschata

FAMILY–MALVACEAE
COMMON NAME–MUSK MALLOW

Origin Asia
Leaves Maple-leaf shaped
Flowers Hibiscus-like, red or pink
Habit Low, spreading, 12 to 18 in
  (30–45cm high)
Season of Bloom Summer
Culture Full sun; will tolerate drought
  and poor soil
Propagation Start seed indoors 8
  weeks before outdoor planting, after
  frost
Utilization Excellent massed in beds
  and borders; good groundcover
Partners Globe amaranth, marigold, pe-
  tunia

Acroclinum roseum

FAMILY–COMPOSITAE
COMMON NAME–EVERLASTING

Origin Western Australia
Leaves Spear-shaped
Flowers Star-shaped, papery in texture,
  1½ to 2 in (3–5cm) wide, mostly
  white and pink
Habit Erect stems up to 2½ ft (75cm)
  high
Season of Bloom Early summer
Culture Full sun
Propagation Sow seed directly into the
  garden after danger of frost is past
Utilization Excellent art flower
Partners Strawflower

Ageratum houstonianum

FAMILY–COMPOSITAE
COMMON NAME–FLOSSFLOWER;
AGERATUM

Origin United States
Leaves Ovate to triangular; ornate; 2 in (5cm) long
Flowers Pink or blue powder-puff
Habit Mounds to 9 in (22cm)
Season of Bloom Spring

Culture Sun; well-drained soil
Propagation Seed
Utilization Good low carpet for borders or edging
Partners Sage; zinnia

Althea rosea

FAMILY–MALVACEAE
COMMON NAME–HOLLYHOCK

Origin China
Leaves Suborbicular; slightly lobed
Flowers Pink or red; full-petaled on tall stems
Habit Erect to 4 ft (1.3m)
Season of Bloom Summer
Culture Deep fertile soil; plenty of moisture
Propagation Seed, barely cover with soil, 70–85°F (21–29°C)
Utilization Good accents in the garden; large flowers
Cultivars 'Majorette'
Partners Brachycome, browallia, calendula

Amaranthus tricolor

FAMILY–AMARANTHACEAE
COMMON NAME–
JOSEPH'S COAT

Origin India
Leaves Brown and red; elliptical; large; 4 in (10cm) long; dense
Flowers Pendant, red seed panicles
Habit Spreading; erect to 4 ft (1.3m)
Season of Bloom Summer, fall
Culture Full sun; tolerates most soil
Propagation Sow seeds directly in garden, 70–85°F (21–29°C)
Utilization Temporary substitute for shrubs against walls, fences
Partners Browallia, calendula, petunia

Anagallis linifolia

FAMILY–PRIMULACEAE
COMMON NAME–PIMPERNEL

Origin Mediterranean region
Leaves Ovate; small; whorled or alternate
Flowers Blue or orange; ¼ in (6mm) across
Habit Prostrate; trailing stems
Season of Bloom Spring, summer
Culture Full sun; light sandy loam
Propagation Sow seeds in garden after frost
Utilization Rock gardens, or use as edgings
Partners Helianthus, salvia, zinnia

Anagallis monelli

FAMILY–PRIMULACEAE
COMMON NAME–
BLUE PIMPERNEL

Origin Mediterranean
Leaves Oval or oblong
Flowers Gentian-blue, star-shaped with yellow 'eye', ¾ in (1.8cm) across
Habit 1 to 2 ft (30–60cm) high, low spreading
Season of Bloom Early summer
Culture Full sun; moist soil
Propagation Sow seed directly into the garden or start indoors 6 weeks before outdoor planting
Utilization Edging and massed bedding
Cultivars 'Pacific Blue'
Partners Diascia

Anchusa capensis

FAMILY–BORAGINACEAE
COMMON NAME–ALKANET;
FORGET-ME-NOT

Origin South Africa
Leaves Lanceolate, narrow, hairy
Flowers Small blue flowers on short stems
Habit Spreading; erect to 12 in (20cm)
Season of Bloom Summer
Culture Sun; well-drained soil
Propagation Sow seed outdoors 4 weeks before last frost, 60°F (15°C)
Utilization Mass plant in beds and borders for best effect
Partners Marigold, petunia

Antirrhinum majus (Hybrids)

FAMILY–SCROPHULARIACEAE
COMMON NAME–SNAPDRAGON

Origin Mediterranean region
Leaves Lanceolate to oblong; 3 in (7.5cm) long
Flowers Blue, white, violet, and pink racemes
Habit Erect to 2 to 4 ft (60cm to 1.2m)
Season of Bloom Spring
Culture Partial sun; lots of water; rich soil; requires feeding
Propagation Sow seed in garden several weeks before frost, 70–85°F (21–29°C)
Utilization Tall varieties good for cut flowers; small plants fine for beds and borders
Cultivars 'Little Darling,' 'Red Flower Carpet,' 'Rocket Mix,' 'Yellow Flower Carpet'
Partners Ageratum, marigold

Arctotis stoechadifolia

FAMILY–COMPOSITAE
COMMON NAME–AFRICAN DAISY

Origin South Africa
Leaves Basal rosettes on alternate stems
Flowers Violet or white; daisylike; 3 in (7.5cm) across
Habit Mounds; grows less than 10 in (25cm) tall
Season of Bloom Summer
Culture Sun; lots of water; requires feeding
Propagation Sow seed in garden after frost. Germination at 60–70°F (15–21°C)
Utilization Good as a cut flower, or as spot color in beds
Partners Antirrhinum, cynoglossum, salvia

Dwarf snapdragons (below) *carpet the ground with a wide variety of flower colors.*

Begonia semperflorens

FAMILY–BEGONIACEAE
COMMON NAME–WAX BEGONIA

Origin Brazil
Leaves Round; large; toothed; dense
Flowers Clusters of pink, red, and white
flowers
Habit Low-growing clumps
Season of Bloom Summer
Culture Shade; rich, moist soil

Propagation Seed must be started 4 to
6 months before last frost—many
people buy pre-starts
Utilization Superb for beds and borders
Cultivars 'Delia,' 'Indian Bridge,'
'Linda,' 'Vodka'
Partners Celosia, marigold, salvia

Bellis perennis

FAMILY–COMPOSITAE
COMMON NAME–ENGLISH DAISY

Origin Europe
Leaves Alternate or basal leaves that
   form a tuft
Flowers White or pink heads 2 in (5cm)
   across
Habit Low-growing
Season of Bloom Spring
Culture Sun; good, well-drained soil
Propagation Sow seed in garden in fall
Utilization Use in front of borders or in
   rock gardens
Partners Cosmos, delphinium,
   helianthus

Brachycome iberidifolia

FAMILY–COMPOSITAE
COMMON NAME–SWAN RIVER
DAISY

Origin Australia, New Zealand
Leaves Pinnately dissected into seg-
   ments
Flowers Blue or rose; daisylike; 2 in
   (5cm) across
Habit Large, massed clumps to 1 ft
   (30cm)
Season of Bloom Summer

Culture Full sun; rich soil
Propagation Sow seed in garden after
   frost, 60–70°F (15–21°C)
Utilization Plant in beds and borders
   for mass display; also good in rock
   gardens
Partners Cosmos, nicotiana, tagetes

Brassica oleracea (Acephala group)

FAMILY–CRUCIFERAE
COMMON NAME–FLOWERING
KALE

Origin Northwestern Europe
Leaves Burgundy-green; frilly; open habit
Flowers Yellow or white
Habit Cabbagelike
Season of Bloom Spring
Culture Partial sun; evenly moist soil
Propagation Sow seeds in garden in late summer
Utilization Borders, interspersed with flowers
Cultivars 'Dynasty Pink'
Partners Dianthus, nicotiana, phlox

Browallia speciosa

FAMILY–SOLANCEAE
COMMON NAME–BUSH VIOLET

Origin Tropical America
Leaves Alternate on stem; small; narrow; pointed
Flowers Blue; trumpet-shaped; 2 in (5cm) across
Habit Spreading to 12 in (30cm)
Season of Bloom Summer
Culture Partial sun; rich, well-drained soil
Propagation Buy young pre-starts
Utilization Use in beds and borders for the vivid blue color
Cultivars 'Marine Bells,' 'Silver Bells'
Partners Coreopsis, cosmos, helenium

Calceolaria herbeohybrida

FAMILY–SCROPHULARIACEAE
COMMON NAME–POCKETBOOK
PLANT

Origin Mexico, Chile, Argentina
Leaves Ovate, toothed, dense
Flowers Yellow with orange spots; profuse; pocketbook shaped
Habit Compact, dense, to 2 ft (60cm)
Season of Bloom Summer
Culture Partial sun; lots of water
Propagation Sow seed or buy pre-starts
Utilization Good container plants, excellent outdoors in borders as edging
Cultivars 'Grandiflora'
Partners Cosmos, tagetes, zinnia

Calceolaria integrifolia

FAMILY–SCROPHULARIACEAE
COMMON NAME–POCKETBOOK
PLANT

Origin Chile
Leaves Oblong; elliptical; serrated; 3 in (7.5cm) long
Flowers Yellow; small; profuse; pouch-like
Habit Low-growing to 3 in (7.5cm)
Season of Bloom Summer
Culture Sun; lots of water
Propagation Sow seed, buy pre-starts
Utilization Good container plant; or for temporary bed color
Partners Cosmos, tagetes, zinnia

Calendula officinalis

FAMILY–COMPOSITAE
COMMON NAME–POT MARIGOLD

Origin Canary Islands
Leaves Oblong, somewhat toothed, dense
Flowers Shades of yellow and orange; powder-puff form
Habit Masses of color to 2 ft (60cm)
Season of Bloom Spring, summer
Culture Sun; fertile, well-drained soil
Propagation Plant seed in garden 1 in (2.5 cm) deep as soon as ground is friable
Utilization Bright flower bed plantings; splendid cut flowers
Cultivars 'Fiesta Mix,' 'Fiesta Yellow'
Partners Ageratum, antirrhinum, centaurea

Callistephus chinensis

FAMILY–COMPOSITAE
COMMON NAME–CHINA ASTER

Origin China
Leaves Alternate, narrow, dense
Flowers White, pink, red, or blue; chrysanthemum-shaped
Habit Rangy to 8 to 12 in (20 to 30cm)
Season of Bloom Fall
Culture Sun; rich, well-drained soil
Propagation Sow indoors 6 weeks before frost; transplant when leaves show; set in garden after frost
Utilization Excellent for flower beds; graceful in floral bouquets
Cultivars 'Pot 'n' Patio'
Partners Cosmos, delphinium, godetia

Campanula medium

FAMILY–CAMPANULACEAE
COMMON NAME–CANTERBURY
BELLS

Origin Mediterranean region
Leaves Rosette of ovate leaves to 10 in
(25cm) long
Flowers Large, white, pink, or blue;
bell-shaped; to 2 in (5cm) across
Habit Erect to 2 ft (60cm)
Season of Bloom Summer, fall
Culture Sun; rich, moist soil
Propagation Sow seed in garden after
last frost or buy pre-starts
Utilization Good in flower borders; at-
tractive cut flowers
Cultivars 'Calycanthema Mix'
Partners Delphinium, impatiens,
nicotiana

Capsicum annuum

FAMILY–SOLANOCEAE
COMMON NAME–PEPPER PLANT

Origin Tropical America
Leaves Lanceolate; 1 to 5 in (2.5 to
10cm) long
Flowers Grow for ornamental purposes
or for red or yellow peppers
Habit Low-growing, bushy, and compact
Season of Bloom Summer
Culture Sun; lots of water
Propagation Seed, or buy pre-starts
Utilization Fine ornamental plant; good
indoors
Partners Use as container plant

Celosia cristata

FAMILY–AMARANTHACEAE
COMMON NAME–COCKSCOMB

Origin Africa
Leaves Alternate, lobed
Flowers Red or yellow; dense spikes in crested shape
Habit Clumps erect to 12 in (30cm)
Season of Bloom Summer

Culture Sun; evenly moist soil
Propagation Sow seed in early summer in garden
Utilization Flower beds, borders
Partners Dianthus, gypsophila

Celosia plumosa

FAMILY–AMARANTHACEAE
COMMON NAME–FEATHER
COCKSCOMB

Origin Africa
Leaves Linear to ovate; often lobed
Flowers Red or yellow; plume-shaped
Habit Erect to 1 ft (30cm)
Season of Bloom Summer
Culture Sun; lots of water
Propagation Sow seed or buy pre-starts
Utilization Use discreetly in gardens as color is blatant; good for drying
Cultivars 'Apricot Brandy,' 'New Look'
Partners Centaurea, gerbera, lobelia, phlox

Centaurea cyanus

FAMILY–COMPOSITAE
COMMON NAME–CORNFLOWER

Origin Mediterranean region
Leaves Pinnate, narrow, cottony, slightly toothed
Flowers Blue; pom-pom shaped; 2 in (5cm) across
Habit Sprawling to 2 ft (60cm), with wiry stems
Season of Bloom Spring, summer
Culture Some sun; will grow in almost any soil
Propagation Sow seed in garden any time in fall
Utilization Effective when massed for color in beds or borders
Partners Marigold, petunia, zinnia

Centaurea moschata

FAMILY–COMPOSITAE
COMMON NAME–SWEET SULTAN

Origin Orient
Leaves Toothed
Flowers Rounded, fluffy flower heads up to 2 in (5cm) across, in pink, white, yellow, and purple
Habit Erect, clump-forming plants grow to 3 ft (1m) high
Season of Bloom Summer
Culture Full sun, cool nights
Propagation Sow seed directly into garden
Utilization Good cut flower
Cultivars 'Imperialis'
Partners Cornflower

Cheiranthus cheiri

FAMILY–CRUCIFERAE
COMMON NAME–WALLFLOWER

Origin Europe
Leaves Narrow, marginal teeth
Flowers Yellow or orange; 1 in (2.5cm) across on terminal spikes
Habit Erect to 2 ft (60cm), with clusters of flowers
Season of Bloom Summer
Culture Partial sun; well-drained soil; add some lime
Propagation Start seed indoors in mid-winter
Utilization Good in rock gardens; mass for late-summer color in flower beds
Partners Iberis, lobelia, phlox, tagetes
NOTE: Perennial grown as half-hardy annual

Chrysanthemum carinatum

FAMILY–COMPOSITAE
COMMON NAME–RAINBOW DAISY,
TRICOLOR DAISY

Origin Morocco
Leaves Toothed like chrysanthemums
Flowers Daisylike, up to 3 in (7.5cm) across with up to three color zones— usually a combination of yellow, white, red, pink, or orange
Habit Erect, clump-forming habit, up to 4 ft (1.2m) high
Season of Bloom Summer
Culture Full sun, well-drained soil
Propagation Sow seed directly into the garden where plants are to bloom
Utilization Good for cutting, mixed borders, and massing in wildflower mixtures
Cultivars 'Court Jesters'
Partners Aster, cosmos, dahlia

Cleome hasslerana

FAMILY–CAPPARACEAE
COMMON NAME–SPIDERFLOWER

Origin Tropical America
Leaves Compound in leaflets
Flowers Clusters of graceful pink or
    white flowers
Habit Handsome clumps; erect to 4 ft
    (1.2m)
Season of Bloom Summer
Culture Some sun; will grow in almost
    any soil
Propagation Sow seed in garden after
    last frost
Utilization Good background plantings;
    excellent as container plants
Partners Antirrhinum, cosmos, zinnia

Coleus X Hybridus

FAMILY–LABIATAE
COMMON NAME–GARDEN
COLEUS

Origin Hybridized from species native
    to Malaysia
Leaves Highly colored; opposite;
    toothed
Flowers Inconspicuous
Habit Dense rosettes
Season of Bloom Spring, summer
Culture Partial shade; well-drained soil
Propagation Start seed indoors 3
    months before spring frost, 70–80°F
    (21–26°C)
Utilization Spectacular for flower beds,
    borders, or indoor boxes
Partners Begonia, impatiens

Consolida ambigua
FAMILY–RANUNCULACEAE
COMMON NAME–LARKSPUR

Origin Europe, Central Asia
Leaves Narrow, divided
Flowers Violet, rose, or pink in erect bunches
Habit Erect to 2 ft (60cm)
Season of Bloom Spring
Culture Partial sun; will grow in any soil

Propagation Sow seeds in garden in early spring
Utilization Excellent bedding plant for the back of the garden; good vertical accent; nice cut flowers
Cultivars 'Blue Elf'
Partners Celosia, gerbera, godetia

Coreopsis tinctoria
FAMILY–COMPOSITAE
COMMON NAME–GOLDEN
COREOPSIS

Origin North America
Leaves Opposite; pinnate; often lobed
Flowers Yellow; daisylike; 2 in (7.5cm) across
Habit Masses to 2 ft (60cm)
Season of Bloom Spring, summer
Culture Some sun; will thrive in almost any soil

Propagation Sow seed in garden in early spring
Utilization Brilliant display in borders; good for cut flowers
Cultivars 'Moonbeam'
Partners Dianthus, gazania, gypsophila

Cosmos bipinnatus

FAMILY–COMPOSITAE
COMMON NAME–COSMOS

Origin Mexico
Leaves Delicate and opposite, cut into
    segments
Flowers Red or pink; daisylike; 1 in
    (2.5cm) across
Habit Handsome clumps; willowy to 4 to
    5 ft (1.2 to 1.5m)
Season of Bloom Spring, summer
Culture Sun; will grow in almost any
    type of soil
Propagation Sow seed in garden after
    last frost
Utilization Use at back of garden beds
    and borders; also good as cut flowers
Cultivars 'Red Sensation,' 'Sensation,'
    'Sunny Gold,' 'Bright Lights'
Partners Godetia, myosotis, phlox

Below: *Tall spikes of Larkspur lend height and color to the garden.*

Cuphea ignea

FAMILY–LYTHRACEAE
COMMON NAME–CIGAR PLANT

Origin Mexico
Leaves Oblong or lanceolate; 3 in (7.5cm) long
Flowers Red, violet, or white; 1 in (2.5cm) long; solitary on slender stalk
Habit Bushy to 18 in (45cm)
Season of Bloom Summer
Culture Sun or shade; will grow in almost any soil
Propagation Sow seed indoors after Christmas
Utilization Colorful edging for walks and borders; good in rock gardens
Partners Cosmos, gerbera, nicotiana

Cynoglossum amabile

FAMILY–BORAGINACEAE
COMMON NAME–CHINESE
FORGET-ME-NOT

Origin East Asia
Leaves Alternate, undivided, rough
Flowers Small and blue in showy clusters
Habit Branching to 2 ft (60cm)
Season of Bloom Summer
Culture Sun or shade; will grow in almost any soil
Propagation Sow seed outdoors as soon as ground can be cultivated
Utilization Useful in beds or borders as accent color
Partners Dyossodia, nicotiana

Dahlia hybrid

FAMILY–COMPOSITAE
COMMON NAME–DAHLIA

Origin Mexico, Guatemala
Leaves Opposite; compound; leaflets or segments; cut or toothed
Flowers Yellow, red, pink, purple, or white; to 5 in (12.5cm) across
Habit Clumps from 2 to 4 ft (60cm to 1.2m)
Season of Bloom Summer, fall
Culture Sun; well-drained soil
Propagation Sow seed indoors 6 to 8 weeks before last frost
Utilization Mass in flower beds; attractive cut flowers
Cultivars 'Bambino Mix,' 'Bouquet,' 'Collorete Mix,' 'Dwarf Elite,' 'Pom-Pom'
Partners Effective in mass by themselves

Dianthus chinensis

FAMILY–CAROPHYLLACEAE
COMMON NAME–CHINA PINK

Origin East Asia
Leaves Opposite, narrow
Flowers Red, white, or pink clusters
Habit Clusters to 18 in (45cm)
Season of Bloom Summer, spring
Culture Full sun; well-drained soil
Propagation Sow seed in garden in fall
Utilization Small dianthus excellent for garden edging; may be massed in beds and borders for accent
Cultivars 'Crimson Charm,' 'Snowfire'
Partners Helianthus, tagetes, zinnia

The large-flowered, double, colorful blooms
of dahlias bring beauty to a garden bed (below).

Diascia barberae

FAMILY–SCROPHULARIACEAE
COMMON NAME–TWINSPUR

Origin South Africa
Leaves Opposite, ovate, toothed
Flowers Pink; ½ in (1.2cm) across on terminal racemes
Habit Masses; willowy to 14 in (35cm)
Season of Bloom Summer
Culture Full sun; well-drained soil
Propagation Start seed indoors 6 weeks before last frost
Utilization Showy in flower beds, doorways
Cultivars 'Ruby Fields'
Partners Browallia, coreopsis, salvia

Dimorphoteca aurantiaca (sinuata)

FAMILY–COMPOSITAE
COMMON NAME–CAPE MARIGOLD

Origin South Africa
Leaves Alternate or basal; somewhat toothed
Flowers Showy; orange or yellow; daisy-like; 2 in (5cm) across
Habit Low-growing clumps to 12 in (30cm)
Season of Bloom Spring, summer

Culture Lots of sun; well-drained soil
Propagation Sow seed outdoors after danger of frost is past
Utilization Good for color in beds and edging; also use for ground cover
Cultivars 'Starshine'
Partners Amaranthus, cosmos, delphinium

Dorotheanthus bellidiflorus

FAMILY–AIZOACEAE
COMMON NAME–ICE PLANT;
LIVINGSTONE DAISY

Origin South Africa
Leaves Opposite, rosettes, succulent
Flowers Rose pink; daisylike; to 2 in (5cm) across; profuse
Habit Low-growing mats to 3 in (7.5cm)
Season of Bloom Summer
Culture Likes sun; will tolerate poor, dry soil
Propagation Sow seed outdoors after danger of frost is past
Utilization Carpets of color for hills; mounds in garden
Partners Artemesia, asclepias, coreopsis

Dyssodia tenuiloba

FAMILY–COMPOSITAE
COMMON NAME–DAHLBERG
DAISY

Origin Mexico
Leaves Alternate, fernlike
Flowers Yellow or orange; 1 in (2.5cm) across on graceful stems
Habit Sprawling mats to 8 in (20cm)
Season of Bloom Summer
Culture Likes sun and dry soil
Propagation Sow seed outdoors after danger of frost is past
Utilization Use in front of borders or for spot color in the garden
Partners Catharanthus, centaurea, gerbera

Emilia javanica

FAMILY–COMPOSITAE
COMMON NAME–
TASSEL FLOWER

Origin Tropics
Leaves Slender, lanceolate
Flowers Buttonlike red-orange flowers up to ½ in (1.2cm) across
Habit Erect
Season of Bloom Early summer
Culture Full sun; prefers cool nights, will tolerate poor soil
Propagation Sow seed directly into the garden
Utilization Good for cutting, mixed annual borders, rock gardens
Cultivars 'Lutea'
Partners Cornflower, poppy

Eschscholzia californica

FAMILY–PAPAVERACEAE
COMMON NAME–CALIFORNIA
POPPY

Origin California
Leaves Dissected, glabrous
Flowers Bright orange; flat-faced
Habit Sprawling to 12 in (30cm)
Season of Bloom Spring
Culture Sun; grows in most soil
Propagation Sow seed in fall
Utilization Good accent in garden, flower beds, drifts
Partners Ageratum, blue salvia, lobelia

Euphorbia marginata

FAMILY–EUPHORBIACEAE
COMMON NAME–
SNOW-ON-THE-MOUNTAIN

Origin North America
Leaves Oblong, blue-green, ooozing a caustic milky sap if cut
Flowers Small, creamy white, inconspicuous; surrounded by ornamental blue-green bracts edged white
Habit Erect, bushy habit
Season of Bloom Mid-summer
Culture Will tolerate high heat, drought, and poor soil
Propagation Sow seed directly into the garden
Utilization Good massed along the house foundation, and singly as an accent in mixed borders
Partners Blue ageratum, blue petunia

Exacum affine

FAMILY–GENTIANIACEAE
COMMON NAME–GERMAN VIOLET

Origin Tropics
Leaves Opposite, stalkless, small, with marginal teeth
Flowers Small pale blue flowers in clusters
Habit Bushy masses of flowers
Season of Bloom Summer, fall

Culture Shade; moist soil
Propagation Seeds need temperatures of 60–65°F (15–18°C)
Utilization Good container plant, tender—will freeze
Partners Best used as a houseplant

Felicia bergerana

FAMILY–COMPOSITAE
COMMON NAME–KINGFISH DAISY

Origin South Africa
Leaves Alternate or opposite; ovate; small
Flowers Blue; daisylike; 1 in (2.5cm) across
Habit Spreading to 6 in (15cm)
Season of Bloom Summer
Culture Full sun; dry soil
Propagation Sow seed indoors in spring; set in garden after frost
Utilization Good edging plant; use in rock gardens
Cultivars 'Alba'
Partners Anemone, centaurea, rudbeckia

Felicia frutescens

FAMILY–COMPOSITAE
COMMON NAME–NONE

Origin South Africa
Leaves Alternate, dark green, fleshy, small
Flowers White to pink; daisylike
Habit Clumps, erect to 12 in (30cm)
Season of Bloom Summer, fall
Culture Sun; dry soil
Propagation Seed in spring
Utilization In flower beds, borders
Partners Gypsophila, matthiola

Fragaria vesca

FAMILY–ROSACEAE
COMMON NAME–ALPINE
STRAWBERRY

Origin North America
Leaves Light green, silky, thin, leaflets
to 2 in (5cm) long
Flowers White flowers; ½ in (1.2cm)
wide on short stems
Habit Sprawling, trailing to 5 in
(12.5cm)

Season of Bloom Summer
Culture Sun; needs plenty of water
Propagation Sow seed indoors in late
winter
Utilization Use as a border plant; good
ground cover
Partners Dwarf zinnia, dwarf marigold

Gaillardia pulchella

FAMILY–COMPOSITAE
COMMON NAME–
BLANKETFLOWER

Origin North America
Leaves Lower leaves spatulate; toothed
or lobed; to 5 in (12.5cm)
Flowers Red with yellow edges; daisy-
like
Habit Leafy, erect, branching to 2 ft
(60cm)
Season of Bloom Summer

Culture Full sun; any garden soil
Propagation Sow seed indoors 4 to 6
weeks before last frost
Utilization Good accent plants; fine cut
flowers
Cultivars 'Goblin,' 'Double Mix'
Partners Cosmos, felicia, rudbeckia

Gaura lindheimeri

FAMILY–ONAGRACEAE
COMMON NAME–NONE

Origin North and South America
Leaves Lanceolate; 2 in (5cm) long
Flowers Pinkish white; 1 in (2.5cm) long; open panicles
Habit Erect but branching to 4 ft (1.2m)
Season of Bloom Spring, summer
Culture Partial sun; will grow in any garden soil
Propagation Start indoors 6 weeks before last frost or buy pre-starts
Utilization Nice branched plant; good for background
Partners Ageratum, browallia, calendula

Gazania linearis

FAMILY–COMPOSITAE
COMMON NAME–NONE

Origin South Africa
Leaves Alternate, basal, feathery
Flowers White to pink; 2 in (5cm) across
Habit Clumps, erect to 24 in (60cm)
Season of Bloom Summer
Culture Sun; well-drained soil
Propagation Seed in spring
Utilization Borders, ground cover, beds
Partners Dianthus, helichrysum, iberis

Gazania ringens

FAMILY–COMPOSITAE
COMMON NAME–NONE

Origin South Africa
Leaves Alternate, basal
Flowers Yellow or orange; daisylike
Habit Low-growing clumps to 12 in (30cm)
Season of Bloom Summer
Culture Needs good drainage; will tolerate dry conditions
Propagation Start seed 6 weeks before last frost
Utilization Use for edging in flower gardens or as ground cover
Cultivars 'Aztec Orange,' 'Aztec Queen,' 'Copper King,' 'Silver Burgundy'
Partners Amaranthus, gerbera, gomphrena

Gerbera jamesonii

FAMILY–COMPOSITAE
COMMON NAME–TRANSVAAL
DAISY

Origin South Africa
Leaves Oblong; hairy; deeply lobed; 10 in (25cm) long
Flowers Scarlet to orange; daisylike; to 4 in (10cm)
Habit Dense clumps to 1 in (2.5cm)
Season of Bloom Summer
Culture Sun; well-drained soil

Propagation Start seeds indoors in late fall at 70–75°F (21–23°C)
Utilization Spectacular garden flower, spot accent
Cultivars 'Happipot'
Partners Iberis, nicotiana, tagetes
NOTE: Perennial grown as half-hardy annual

Godetia (Clarkia)
amoena

FAMILY–ONAGRACEAE
COMMON NAME–
FAREWELL-TO-SPRING

Origin North America
Leaves Alternate, narrow, toothed
Flowers White marked with red; clusters
Habit Clusters to 2 ft (60cm)
Season of Bloom Spring, summer
Culture Partial sun; well-drained soil
Propagation Sow seed in garden in spring
Utilization Showy additions to flower beds; good for cut flowers
Partners Browallia, nicotiana, tagetes

Gomphrena globosa

FAMILY–AMARANTHACEAE
COMMON NAME–GLOBE
AMARANTH

Origin Tropics
Leaves Oblong on elliptical units; hairy margins
Flowers Heads of red, pink, or white; 1 in (2.5cm) across
Habit Mounds to 12 in (30cm)
Season of Bloom Summer

Culture Sun; well-drained soil
Propagation Start seeds indoors 6 weeks before last spring frost
Utilization Plant in high windy places; good for cut flowers, drying
Partners Nicotiana, tagetes, zinnia

Helianthus annuus

FAMILY–COMPOSITAE
COMMON NAME–COMMON
SUNFLOWER

Origin North America
Leaves Alternate, cordate
Flowers Yellow; large; daisylike; to 10 in (25cm) across
Habit Clumps to 6 ft (2m)
Season of Bloom Summer
Culture Tolerates shade; will grow in almost any soil
Propagation Sow seed outdoors when danger of frost is past
Utilization Good temporary hedges and screen
Cultivars 'Sunburst,' 'Sunrose,' 'Teddy Bear'
Partners Begonia, celosia, phlox

Helichrysum bracteatum—(yellow, white, red)

FAMILY–COMPOSITAE
COMMON NAME–EVERLASTING;
STRAWFLOWER

Origin Australia
Leaves Green, oblong, long, glabrous
Flowers Yellow, red, salmon, or white; true flowers, 1 to 2 in (2.5 to 5cm) across, in center of colorful branches
Habit Great clumps to 1 ft (30cm)
Season of Bloom Spring, summer
Culture Sun; will grow in average soil
Propagation Start plants indoors 6 to 8 weeks before last frost
Utilization Good for dried bouquets; nice accent or edging plant
Cultivars 'Diamond Head,' 'Moe's Gold'
Partners Arctotis, centaura, salvia

Heliotropium
arborescens

FAMILY–BORAGINACEAE
COMMON NAME–HELIOTROPE

Origin Peru
Leaves Alternate; large; usually hairy
Flowers Small purple flowers; clusters
Habit Clumps to 3 ft (1m)
Season of Bloom Summer, fall
Culture Some sun; well-drained soil
Propagation Start seed indoors in con-
     tainers or buy pre-starts
Utilization Good for flower borders or
     as spot accent
Cultivars 'Black Prince'
Partners Browallia, centaurea, mirabilis

Below: *Various shades of pink of different
impatiens varieties stand out in the shade of a large tree.*

Iberis umbellatum

FAMILY–CRUCIFERAE
COMMON NAME–GLOBE
CANDYTUFT

Origin Europe
Leaves Alternate; divided or undivided
Flowers Small, pink or violet; in dense umbels
Habit Erect to 1 ft (30cm)
Season of Bloom Spring
Culture Sun; will grow in most soils

Propagation Sow seed outdoors in late summer in temperate zones; sow indoors in severe climates
Utilization Good for flower borders and edging
Cultivars 'Dwarf Fairy'
Partners Antirrhinum, marigold

Impatiens balsamina

FAMILY–BALSAMINACEA
COMMON NAME–BALSAM

Origin China and Malaysia
Leaves Dark green, lanceolate
Flowers Mostly double-flowered, borne in the leaf axils along erect, succulent stems in white, pink, red, and purple, 2 in (6cm) across
Habit Erect, bushy
Season of Bloom Mid-summer
Culture Light shade; will tolerate high heat and humidity; prefers moist, humus-rich soil
Propagation Sow seed directly into garden after danger of frost is past, or start seed indoors 6 weeks before outdoor planting
Utilization Mostly used massed in light shade
Cultivars 'Camellia-flowered'
Partners Browallia, coleus, impatiens, wax begonias

Impatiens wallerana

FAMILY–BALSAMINACEAE
COMMON NAME–IMPATIENS

Origin Asia
Leaves Lanceolate; ovate to elliptical
Flowers Red, pink, or orange; open-faced; 1 in (2.5cm) across
Habit Bushy to 2 ft (60cm)
Season of Bloom Summer, fall

Culture Shade; well-drained soil
Propagation Sow seed or buy pre-starts
Utilization Good long bloom in flower beds; good for terrace gardens
Partners Celosia, nicotiana, tagetes

Ipomoea purpurea

FAMILY–CONVOLVULACEAE
COMMON NAME–MORNING
GLORY

Origin Tropical America
Leaves Generally stalked with leaflets; ovate; 5 in (12.5cm) long
Flowers Pink or blue; funnel-shaped
Habit Vining to 8 ft (2.4m)
Season of Bloom Fall
Culture Sun; moist, well-drained soil
Propagation Sow seed outdoors after danger of frost is past
Utilization Lovely hedges or screens
Cultivars 'Early Call,' 'Heavenly Blue'
Partners Effective by itself

Iresine herbstii

FAMILY–AMARANTHACEAE
COMMON NAME–BLOODLEAF

Origin South America
Leaves Deep purple-red; oval; large; notched
Flowers White; inconspicuous
Habit Erect shrubs to 4 ft (1.2m)
Season of Bloom Summer
Culture Partial sun; thrives in average soil
Propagation Cuttings in winter or spring
Utilization Very effective in group plantings or in garden beds
Partners Browallia, coreopsis, roses

Lantana camara

FAMILY–VERBENACEAE
COMMON NAME–YELLOW SAGE

Origin Tropical America
Leaves Opposite, hairy, toothed
Flowers Orange or lavender; terminal clusters
Habit Spreading; bushy to 2 ft (60cm)
Season of Bloom Summer, fall
Culture Partial sun; moist soil
Propagation Start seed indoors in late winter
Utilization Good background plant or accent
Cultivars 'Christine Red'
Partners Gazania, phlox, salvia

Lathyrus odoratus

FAMILY–LEGUMINOSAE
COMMON NAME–SWEET PEA

Origin Italy
Leaves In pairs; elliptical; to 2 in (5cm) long
Flowers White or pink; 2 in (5cm) across; in clusters
Habit Climber, vining to 6 ft (2m)
Season of Bloom Spring

Culture Sun; rich, deep soil; needs moisture
Propagation Sow seed as soon as soil can be worked
Utilization Good for screens, trellises; attractive cut flowers
Partners Ageratum, celosia, nicotiana

Limonium sinuatum

FAMILY–PLUMBAGINACEAE
COMMON NAME–SEA LAVENDER;
STATICE

Origin Mediterranean region
Leaves Alternate on stems or basal rosettes
Flowers Blue, lavender, rose, or white; small; in tight clusters
Habit Bushy to 20 in (50cm)
Season of Bloom Summer, fall

Culture Sun; well-drained soil
Propagation Start seed indoors 8 weeks before last spring frost
Utilization Excellent cut and dried flowers
Partners Ageratum, brachycome, browallia

Lisianthus (Eustoma) grandiflorum

FAMILY–GENTIANACEAE
COMMON NAME–PRAIRIE
GENTIAN

Origin West Indies, Mexico
Leaves Ovate or lanceolate
Flowers Purple or white; to 1 in (2.5cm) long
Habit Branching to 4 ft (1.2m)
Season of Bloom Summer, fall
Culture Sun; well-drained soil
Propagation Sow seed in garden after last frost
Utilization Bedding plant
Partners Coreopsis, helianthus, limonium

Lobelia erinus

FAMILY–LOBELIACEAE
COMMON NAME–LOBELIA

Origin South Africa
Leaves Alternate; sometimes in rosettes; ovate; serrated
Flowers Blue or violet; ½ in (1.2cm) long on slender stalks
Habit Erect or trailing from 3 to 8 in (7.5 to 20cm)
Season of Bloom Spring
Culture Partial shade; well-drained soil

Propagation Start seed indoors in late winter
Utilization Use in borders or edging; good for hanging baskets
Cultivars 'Blue Cascade,' 'Blue Moon,' 'Cambridge Blue,' 'Crystal Palace,' 'Dark Cobalt'
Partners Alyssum, celosia, petunia

Lobularia maritima

FAMILY–CRUCIFERAE
COMMON NAME–SWEET ALYSSUM

Origin Mediterranean region
Leaves Alternate with border margin
Flowers Tiny, white or lilac; in umbels
Habit Spreading; masses to 1 ft (30cm)
Season of Bloom Spring, summer
Culture Sun; will thrive in almost any soil

Propagation Sow seeds in early spring in garden 6 weeks before last frost
Utilization Superior edging plant
Cultivars 'Color Carpet Mix,' 'Rose O' Day'
Partners Petunia, verbena, zinnia

Lunaria annua 'Honesty'

FAMILY–CRUCIFERAE
COMMON NAME–MONEY PLANT

Origin Southern Europe
Leaves Alternate, stalked, oval
Flowers White flowers in large, showy racemes
Habit Erect to 36 in (1m)
Season of Bloom Summer

Culture Evenly moist soil; partial shade
Propagation Sow seed indoors in spring
Utilization Use in dried flower arrangements
Partners Delphinium, dianthus

Matricaria recutita

FAMILY–COMPOSITAE
COMMON NAME–CHAMOMILE

Origin Europe, Asia
Leaves Finely cut and dissected
Flowers Yellow; daisylike; 1 in (2.5cm) across
Habit Spreading to 2 ft (60cm)
Season of Bloom Summer
Culture Sun; well-drained soil
Propagation Sow seed in early spring
Utilization Good bedding or edging plant; mass of color
Partners Sage, salpiglossis

Matthiola incana

FAMILY–CRUCIFERAE
COMMON NAME–STOCK

Origin Europe, Asia
Leaves Alternate, without marginal teeth
Flowers White, blue, or purple in loose clusters to 1 in (2.5cm) across
Habit Vertical, densely flowered to 2 ft (60cm)
Season of Bloom Spring, summer
Culture Sun; well-drained soil
Propagation Sow seed outdoors in very early spring
Utilization Excellent for flower beds, or for fragrance
Cultivars 'Brompton Mix,' 'Excelsior Red,' 'Rose Midget'
Partners Cosmos, larkspur, zinnia

Matthiola longipetala
bicornis

FAMILY–CRUCIFERAE
COMMON NAME–NIGHT-SCENTED
STOCK

Origin Mediterranean
Leaves Slender, pointed, lanceolate
Flowers Small, four-petalled, mostly in white, pink, and purple; highly fragrant, especially in the evening
Habit Clump-forming, loose, airy habit, to 3 ft (1m) high
Season of Bloom Summer
Culture Prefers cool nights, full sun or light shade, humus-rich soil
Propagation Sow seed directly into the garden; will tolerate crowding
Utilization Mostly used massed near the house where its evening fragrance can be appreciated
Partners Combines well with most tall-growing annuals in mixed borders

Melampodium
paludosum

FAMILY–COMPOSITAE
COMMON NAME–BUSH ZINNIA

Origin South America
Leaves Slender, pointed, bright green
Flowers Small, zinnia-like, yellow, ½ in (1.2cm) across, borne continuously in profusion
Habit Bushy, dome-shaped, up to 3 ft (1m) high
Season of Bloom Summer
Culture Full sun; will tolerate high heat, drought, and poor soil as long as it drains well
Propagation Sow seed directly into the garden after danger of frost is past
Utilization Mostly used as a temporary flowering background "hedge"
Partners Petunia, red zinnia, scarlet sage, snapdragon

Mimulus guttatus

FAMILY–SCROPHULARIACEAE
COMMON NAME–
MONKEYFLOWER

Origin North, South America
Leaves Opposite; sometimes hairy;
   dense
Flowers Showy orange and yellow; dots
   on lips
Habit Small, shrublike to 18 in (45cm)
Season of Bloom Spring, summer
Culture Likes sun; will tolerate wet soil
Propagation Sow seeds indoors or buy
   pre-starts
Utilization Good bedding plant
Cultivars 'Malibu Orange,' 'Malibu
   Yellow'
Partners Amaranthus, tagetes, zinnia

Mirabilis jalapa

FAMILY–NYCTAGINACEAE
COMMON NAME–FOUR-O'CLOCK
FLOWER

Origin Peru
Leaves Opposite, generally stalked,
   glabrous
Flowers Red or yellow; tubular
Habit Spreading; bushy to 2 ft (60cm)
Season of Bloom Spring, summer
Culture Sun; well-drained soil
Propagation Start seed indoors 6
   weeks before last frost
Utilization Background plant, bedding
   plant
Partners Browallia, gaillardia, phlox

Myosotis sylvatica

FAMILY–BORAGINACEAE
COMMON NAME–FORGET-ME-NOT

Origin Europe, Asia
Leaves Alternate, without teeth
Flowers Blue, sometimes pink; tiny
Habit Bushy to 12 in (30cm)
Season of Bloom Spring, summer
Culture Partial shade; any soil
Propagation Sow seed outdoors in
   early spring
Utilization Excellent edging and border
   plant, good for cut flowers
Cultivars 'Blue Bird'
Partners Allysum, arabis, viola

Nemesia strumosa
'Rainbow'

FAMILY–SCROPHULARIACEAE
COMMON NAME–NONE

Origin Hybrid (South Africa)
Leaves In pairs; lanceolate
Flowers Orange; to 1 in (2.5cm) across
   in clusters
Habit Spreading; bushy to 2 ft (60cm)
Season of Bloom Spring, summer
Culture Sun; moist soil
Propagation Start seed indoors in mid-
   winter, or buy pre-starts
Utilization Good edging plant; fine cut
   flower
Cultivars 'Carnival'
Partners Celosia, centaurea, gerbera

Nicandra physalodes

FAMILY–SOLANACAEA
COMMON NAME–SHOO-FLY
PLANT

Origin Peru

Leaves Bright green, spearshaped, indented

Flowers Blue with white throat, resembling morning glories, followed by decorative seed cases resembling Chinese lanterns

Habit Bushy, erect, to 2 ft (60 cm)

Season of Bloom Summer

Culture Full sun; will tolerate poor soil

Propagation Start seeds indoors six weeks before planting outdoors after danger of frost is past

Utilization Containers, mixed beds and borders; flowers are repellent to many insects, especially flies

Cultivars 'Violacea'

Partners Popular mixed with annual herbs, such as basil, in herb gardens

Nicotiana alata

FAMILY–SOLANACEAE
COMMON NAME–TOBACCO
PLANT

Origin Tropical America

Leaves Ovate, to 10 in (25cm) long

Flowers White, pink, or red; star-shaped on tall stems

Habit Erect but rangy to 2 ft (60cm)

Season of Bloom Summer

Culture Sun or shade; lots of water

Propagation Sow seed or buy pre-starts

Utilization Useful for flower borders; fragrant cut flowers

Cultivars 'Niki-Pink,' 'Niki-Red,' 'White Domino'

Partners Delphinium, gaillardia, gerbera

Nierembergia hippomanica violacea

FAMILY–SOLANACEAE
COMMON NAME–CUPFLOWER

Origin Tropical America
Leaves Alternate, smooth edges
Flowers Violet-blue with yellow throat; small; profuse
Habit Ground cover, creeper, to 10 in (25cm)
Season of Bloom Summer
Culture Some sun; moist soil
Propagation Sow seed indoors in early spring or buy pre-starts
Utilization Good for show in open border or rock garden
Cultivars 'Purple Robe'
Partners Petunia, verbena

Nigella damascena

FAMILY–RANUNCULACEAE
COMMON NAME–LOVE-IN-A-MIST

Origin Mediterranean region
Leaves Palmately parted, threadlike
Flowers Blue, pink, or rose; in bracts to 1 in (2.5cm) across
Habit Clumps, branching to 2 ft (60cm)
Season of Bloom Spring
Culture Full sun; moist soil

Propagation Sow seed or buy pre-starts
Utilization Good cut flowers; use as hill accent or in floral border
Cultivars 'Miss Jekyll'
Partners Gaillardia, gerbera, gypsophila

Nolana paradoxa

FAMILY–NOLANACEAE
COMMON NAME–NONE

Origin Chile, Peru
Leaves Ovate; fleshy
Flowers Blue with yellow throat
Habit Decumbent to 8 ft (2.4m)
Season of Bloom Summer

Culture Some sun; well-drained soil
Propagation Seed or buy pre-starts
Utilization Good accent plant; use in low mounds for hills
Partners Marigold, nicotiana, zinnia

Ocimum basilicum

FAMILY–LABIATAE
COMMON NAME–SWEET BASIL

Origin Africa
Leaves Dark green or purple; ovate or elliptical; toothed; 3 to 5 in (7.5 to 12.5cm) long
Flowers Small, white or purple; on panicles
Habit Dense to 2 ft (60cm)
Season of Bloom Summer

Culture Full sun; does well in light sandy soil
Propagation Sow seed or buy pre-starts
Utilization Good foliage plant in beds and borders; include in herb beds
Partners Alyssum, begonia

Papaver commutatum

FAMILY–PAPAVERACEAE
COMMON NAME–FLANDER'S
FIELD POPPY

Origin Europe
Leaves Toothed, slender, hairy
Flowers Red, satiny, sometimes with
   black markings at the petal base, up
   to 3 in. (7.5cm) across
Habit Clump-forming, 2 ft. (60cm) high
Season of Bloom Early summer
Culture Full sun; will tolerate poor with
   good drainage; likes cool nights
Propagation Sow seed directly into the
   garden since plants will not tolerate
   transplanting
Utilization Mixed borders and wild-
   flower meadow mixtures
Cultivars 'Lady Bird'
Partners Cornflower, lavender

Papaver nudicaule

FAMILY–PAPAVARACEAE
COMMON NAME–ICELAND POPPY

Origin Europe, Asia
Leaves Basal leaves; deeply segmented
   and hairy; dense
Flowers Red or violet, vividly colored,
   solitary on long stalks; cup-shaped
Habit Sprawling clumps, erect to 12 in
   (30cm)
Season of Bloom Spring

Culture Sun; light, well-drained soil
Propagation Sow seeds in garden or
   buy pre-starts
Utilization Most effective when massed
   in beds by themselves
Partners Ageratum, antirrhinum,
   brachycome

Papaver rhoeas

FAMILY–PAPAVARACEAE
COMMON NAME–CORN POPPY;
SHIRLEY POPPY

Origin Europe, Asia
Leaves Irregularly pinnate to 6 in (15cm) long
Flowers Scarlet or purple; large; cup-shaped
Habit Branching and wiry to 2 ft (60cm)
Season of Bloom Spring

Culture Sun; light well-drained soil
Propagation Sow seed or buy pre-starts
Utilization Great when massed by themselves; good cut flower
Partners Anchusa, centaurea, salpiglossis

Pelargonium peltatum

FAMILY–GERANIACEAE
COMMON NAME–IVY GERANIUM

Origin Brazil
Leaves Peltate, ovate, lobed, 2 to 3 in (5 to 7.5cm) across
Flowers Pink or white; small; plentiful
Habit Trailing to 3 ft (1m)
Season of Bloom Fall

Culture Partial sun; lots of water
Propagation Cuttings
Utilization For hanging baskets in gardens, porches
Partners Best in containers

Pelargonium X domesticum

FAMILY–GERANIACEAE
COMMON NAME–MARTHA
WASHINGTON GERANIUM

Origin Hybrid developed from species native to South Africa
Leaves Mostly lobed and toothed
Flowers White, pink, red, or purple with markings
Habit Bushy clumps
Season of Bloom Summer, fall
Culture Lots of water, sun
Propagation Cuttings
Utilization Good container or bedding plants
Partners Best in containers

Pelargonium X hortorum

FAMILY–GERANIACEAE
COMMON NAME–ZONAL
GERANIUM

Origin Hybrid developed from species native to South Africa
Leaves Rounded; cordate; scalloped; 3 to 5 in (7.5 to 10cm) across; zoned or variegated
Flowers Red, pink, salmon, or white
Habit Bushy to 3 ft (1m)
Season of Bloom Summer
Culture Sun; lots of water
Propagation Cuttings
Utilization Fine bedding plants; good for containers
Cultivars 'Carefree Salmon,' 'Penny Irene'
Partners Best in containers

Petunia X hybrida

FAMILY–SOLANACEAE
COMMON NAME–PETUNIA

Origin Argentina
Leaves Large, soft; dense
Flowers All colors except black; large; small; fringed; wavy
Habit Sprawling or erect to 12 in (30cm)
Season of Bloom Spring, summer
Culture Sun; lots of water

Propagation Buy pre-starts
Utilization Good massed by themselves, or use for edging and borders
Cultivars 'Blue Flash,' 'Flare,' 'Rare Madness,' 'Red Cascade,' 'Summer Madness,' 'Super Cascade'
Partners Coreopsis, salvia

Phlox drummondii

FAMILY–POLEMONIACEAE
COMMON NAME–ANNUAL PHLOX

Origin North America
Leaves Lanceolate
Flowers Showy lilac, purple, or pink; in clusters
Habit Spreading; semierect to 18 in (45cm)
Season of Bloom Summer, fall
Culture Well-drained soil; full sun

Propagation Sow seed outdoors after last frost, or buy pre-starts
Utilization Make handsome beds and wide borders; good in rock gardens
Cultivars 'Blue Beauty,' 'Dwarf Beauty Mix,' 'Petticoat,' 'Salmon Beauty'
Partners Coreopsis, nicotiana, salvia

Polygonum capitatum

FAMILY–POLYGONACEAE
COMMON NAME–KNOTWEED

Origin Himalayas
Leaves Opposite, simple, elliptical
Flowers Pink; in dense heads
Habit Sprawling; trailing to 10 in (25cm)
Season of Bloom Summer
Culture Sun; well-drained soil
Propagation Sow seed indoors in early
   spring
Utilization Good edging plant; also use
   for ground cover
Partners ageratum, anchusa, phlox

Portulaca grandiflora

FAMILY–PORTULACACEAE
COMMON NAME–ROSE MOSS

Origin Brazil
Leaves Alternate, small, thick; spoon-
   shaped
Flowers White or pink; to 1 in (2.5cm)
Habit Sprawling; trailing to 10 in (25cm)
Season of Bloom Summer, fall
Culture Sun; will tolerate dry condi-
   tions
Propagation Sow seed indoors 8 weeks
   before last frost
Utilization Good for dry banks and rock
   gardens
Cultivars 'Magic Carpet,' 'Sunnyside
   Coral'
Partners Antirrhinum, phlox, tagetes

Primula X obconica

FAMILY–PRIMULACEAE
COMMON NAME–GERMAN
PRIMULA

Origin China
Leaves Ovate, elliptical, scalloped
Flowers Lilac or pink; in rounded heads
Habit Dense clumps to 1 ft (30cm)
Season of Bloom Spring
Culture Partial shade; well-drained soil
Propagation Cool seeds and start indoors in fall
Utilization Useful in rock gardens and borders
Cultivars 'Crescendo'
Partners Coreopsis, gerbera
NOTE: Perennial treated as annual. Leaves can cause rash on skin.

Rudbeckia hirta

FAMILY–COMPOSITAE
COMMON NAME–CORNFLOWER;
BLACK-EYED SUSAN

Origin North America
Leaves Alternate or lobed; lanceolate
Flowers Yellow; daisylike
Habit Masses to 2 ft (60cm)
Season of Bloom Summer, fall
Culture Partial shade; average to dry soil
Propagation Sow outdoors in warm soil, buy pre-starts
Utilization Good for beds and borders; also used as cut flowers
Cultivars 'Marmalade'
Partners Amaranthus, bellis, campanula

Salpiglossis sinuata

FAMILY–SOLANACEAE
COMMON NAME–
PAINTED-TONGUE FLOWER

Origin Chile
Leaves Lanceolate; margins wavy or slightly serrated
Flowers Scarlet, blue, or yellow; on wiry stems
Habit Clumps branching to 2 ft (60cm)
Season of Bloom Fall
Culture Partial shade; well-drained soil
Propagation Sow seeds indoors in early spring or buy pre-starts
Utilization Good cut flowers; excellent background plants
Cultivars 'Bolero,' 'Splash'
Partners Marigold, petunia

Salvia farinacea

FAMILY–LABIATAE
COMMON NAME–CUP SAGE

Origin Tropical America
Leaves In pairs; oval or lanceolate
Flowers Blue flowers in dense racemes
Habit Erect to 3 ft (1m)
Season of Bloom Spring, summer
Culture Sun; fertile, well-drained soil
Propagation Sow seed outdoors after last frost
Utilization Handsome in flower beds or for background plantings; good cut flowers
Cultivars 'Argent White,' 'Victoria,' 'Wrightii'
Partners Coreopsis, phlox, primula
NOTE: Perennial grown as half-hardy annual

Salvia splendens

FAMILY–LABIATAE
COMMON NAME–SCARLET SAGE

Origin Brazil
Leaves Opposite; in pairs; oval or lanceo-
late; often hairy; marginal teeth
Flowers Scarlet plumes
Habit Dense to 2 ft (60cm)
Season of Bloom Summer
Culture Sun; well-drained soil
Propagation Start seed indoors or out-
doors when soil is warm
Utilization Excellent bedding plant;
background color
Cultivars 'Flamenco'
Partners Petunia

Sanvitalia procumbens

FAMILY–COMPOSITAE
COMMON NAME–CREEPING
ZINNIA

Origin Mexico
Leaves Oval to lanceolate; 2 in (5cm)
long
Flowers Yellow; small; terminal heads;
profuse
Habit Creeping to 6 in (15cm)
Season of Bloom Summer, fall
Culture Sun; well-drained soil
Propagation Sow seed in garden after
danger of frost is past
Utilization Edgings and rock gardens
Cultivars 'Goldbird'
Partners Centaurea, gerbera, phlox

Satureja hortensis

FAMILY–LABIATAE
COMMON NAME–SAVORY

Origin Mediterranean region
Leaves Oval or lanceolate; toothed
(grown for its flavorful leaves)
Flowers White or pink; ½ in (1.2cm)
across
Habit Grows to 6 to 12 in (15 to 30cm)
Season of Bloom Summer

Culture Sun; will tolerate dry soil
Propagation Sow seed outdoors in
early spring
Utilization Use in herb gardens; good
for edgings
Partners Antirrhinum, gerbera, phlox

Scabiosa atropurpurea

FAMILY–DIPSACACEAE
COMMON NAME–PINCUSHION
FLOWER

Origin Europe, Asia
Leaves Oval or lanceolate; lobed
Flowers Purple, pink, or white; 2 in
(5cm) heads
Habit Variable, but usually erect to 2 ft
(60cm)
Season of Bloom Summer, fall
Culture Sun; well-drained soil
Propagation Sow seed
Utilization Nice cut flowers; good for
flower beds
Partners Foliage plants

Schizanthus pinnatus

FAMILY–SOLANACEAE
COMMON NAME–BUTTERFLY
FLOWER

Origin Chile
Leaves Broad, lanceolate, fernlike
Flowers White, red, or rose clusters
Habit Spreading to 4 ft (1.2m)
Season of Bloom Spring
Culture Partial sun; well-drained soil
Propagation Sow seed indoors in
      winter
Utilization Prized for profuse flowering;
      good cut flowers
Cultivars 'Angel Wings,' 'Hit Parade'
Partners Petunia, portulaca, verbena

Senecio X hybridus

FAMILY–COMPOSITAE
COMMON NAME–CINERARIA

Origin Hybrid
Leaves Alternate or basal; usually large
Flowers Red, violet, blue, or white;
      daisylike; clusters of flowers
Habit Bushy and dense from 10 in to
      2 ft (20 to 60cm)
Season of Bloom Summer, fall
Culture Partial shade; lots of water
Propagation Buy pre-starts
Utilization For shaded patios and ter-
      races; good container plants
Partners Calendula, portulaca

Tagetes erecta

FAMILY–COMPOSITAE
COMMON NAME–MARIGOLD;
AFRICAN MARIGOLD

Origin Mexico to Argentina
Leaves Opposite, dissected, scented
Flowers Showy flower heads of white, red, orange, and many other colors
Habit Bushy, stray, dense, many flowers
Season of Bloom Spring, summer, fall
Culture Almost any kind of soil, plenty of moisture
Propagation Buy pre-starts
Utilization Marigolds work almost anywhere in the garden—in beds, borders, terraces, and so on
Cultivars 'Baby Boy,' 'Bonanza Yellow,' 'Dainty Marietta,' 'Disco,' 'Golden Gem,' 'Gold Boy,' 'Lemon Gem,' 'Nugget,' 'Paprika,' 'Queen Sophia,' 'Scarlet Sophie'
Partners Allysum, lobelia, nierembergia

Tagetes patula

FAMILY–COMPOSITAE
COMMON NAME–FRENCH
MARIGOLD

Origin Mexico
Leaves Toothed, spicy odor
Flowers Yellow, orange, gold, or rusty-red, bi-colors
Habit Bushy, 6–18 inches
Season of Bloom Summer
Culture Full sun; will tolerate poor soil
Propagation Sow seeds directly or start 6 weeks before outdoor planting, after frost
Utilization Beds, borders, containers
Cultivars 'Boy O'Boy,' 'Petite,' 'Jamie,' 'Queen Sophia'
Partners Alyssum, ageratum, dwarf zinnia, petunia

Thunbergia alata

FAMILY–ACANTHACEAE
COMMON NAME–BLACK-EYED
SUSAN

Origin Africa
Leaves Opposite, arrow-shaped
Flowers Showy orange with purple
    throat
Habit Vine twining to 6 ft (2m)
Season of Bloom Summer
Culture Sun; grows in most soils
Propagation Sow seed in garden in
    early spring
Utilization Excellent for baskets and
    ground covers or on trellises, fences,
    or walls
Partners Effective by itself

Tithonia rotundifolia

FAMILY–COMPOSITAE
COMMON NAME–MEXICAN
SUNFLOWER

Origin Mexico, Central America
Leaves Alternate, oval, deeply lobed or
    round-toothed
Flowers Orange or red; daisylike flower
    heads
Habit Clumps, erect to 4 ft (1.2m)
Season of Bloom Fall
Culture Sun; grows in almost any soil
Propagation Sow seeds indoors 8
    weeks before last spring frost
Utilization Good background plant; can
    be used as temporary hedge
Cultivars 'Goldfinger'
Partners Achillea, bellis, campanula

Nasturtium flowers (below), *always bright in color, may be red, yellow, or orange, and bloom on vining or bushy plants.*

Torenia fournieri

FAMILY–SCROPHULARIACEAE
COMMON NAME–WISHBONE
FLOWER

Origin Africa
Leaves Stalked, tinted, oval
Flowers Blue with purplish throats; in clusters
Habit Compact clumps, erect to 12 in (30cm)
Season of Bloom Summer, fall
Culture Partial shade; warm, moist soil
Propagation Sow seed indoors 12 weeks before last frost
Utilization Use in garden borders; also good in pots and hanging baskets
Partners Begonia, impatiens

Tropaeoelum majus

FAMILY–TROPAEOLACEAE
COMMON NAME–NASTURTIUM

Origin South America
Leaves Bright green, rounded; veins radiate from center
Flowers Showy; orange or crimson; solitaires
Habit Rambling, spreading, climbing to 8 ft (2.4m)
Season of Bloom Summer, fall

Culture Likes sun; will grow in almost any soil
Propagation Sow seeds in garden 2 weeks before last frost
Utilization Excellent cover for trellises, fences, and rocks
Partners Coreopsis, marigold, papaver

Venidium fastuosum

FAMILY–COMPOSITAE
COMMON NAME–CAPE DAISY;
MARCH-OF-THE-VELDT

Origin South Africa
Leaves Alternate, fernlike, deeply cut
Flowers Yellow; densely petaled; daisy-like; to 4 in (10cm)
Habit Sprawling and scandent to 2 ft (60cm)
Season of Bloom Summer
Culture Sun; likes dry soil
Propagation Sow seed indoors in early spring
Utilization Good addition to border; attractive cut flowers
Partners Brachycome, browallia, zinnia

Verbena X hybrida

FAMILY–VERBENACEAE
COMMON NAME–NONE

Origin North America
Leaves Usually lobed and toothed
Flowers White, lilac, purple, or red
Habit Upright or trailing to 12 in (30cm)
Season of Bloom Spring, summer
Culture Partial sun; well-drained soil
Propagation Sow seed or buy pre-starts
Utilization Good to cover banks, hills; satisfactory for edgings
Cultivars 'Polaris,' 'Romantic Burgundy,' 'St. Paul,' 'Springtime'
Partners Brachycome, petunia, salvia

Viola tricolor

FAMILY–VIOLACEAE
COMMON NAME–
JOHNNY-JUMP-UP

Origin Europe
Leaves Basal, ovate, crenate, deeply lobed
Flowers Tricolored, of yellow, purple-red, and violet-blue; open-faced
Habit Bushy, low-growing
Season of Bloom Spring, summer
Culture Sun; needs a moist, fertile soil
Propagation Start seed indoors 10 weeks before last spring frost
Utilization Brilliant bases of color in border and edgings
Cultivars 'Bambino Mix,' 'Ruby Queen'
Partners Alyssum, iberis
NOTE: Perennial treated as hardy annual

Viola X wittrockiana

FAMILY–VIOLACEAE
COMMON NAME–PANSY

Origin Hybrid
Leaves Ovate, elliptical, dense
Flowers Various colors, including purple, blue, maroon, orange; open; 2 to 5 in (5 to 12.5cm) across
Habit Leafy, dense, to 9 in (22.5cm)
Season of Bloom Spring, summer
Culture Sun; needs fertile soil

Propagation Sow seed indoors 10 weeks before last spring frost or buy pre-starts
Utilization Fine edging plant
Cultivars 'Red Wing'
Partners Nicotiana, salvia
NOTE: Perennial treated as hardy annual

Zinnia angustifolia

FAMILY–COMPOSITAE
COMMON NAME–ZINNIA

Origin Mexico, Chile
Leaves Linear to 3 in (7.5cm) long
Flowers Yellow or orange heads 1½ in
  (4cm) across
Habit Leafy, densely flowered, to 16 in
  (40cm)
Season of Bloom Spring, summer, fall

Culture Sun; good, fertile soil
Propagation Sow seed 10 weeks before
  last spring frost or buy pre-starts
Utilization Decorative in borders, ar-
  rangements, or edgings
Cultivars 'Classic'
Partners Gypsophila, lobelia, phlox

Zinnia elegans

FAMILY–COMPOSITAE
COMMON NAME–COMMON
ZINNIA

Origin Mexico
Leaves Dense, linear
Flowers Almost all colors except blue
Habit Densely flowered, grows to 2 ft
  (60cm)
Season of Bloom Summer, fall
Culture Sun; fertile soil

Propagation Start seed indoors at least
  6 weeks before plants will be put outside or buy pre-starts
Utilization Flower beds; terraces
Cultivars 'Cut n' Come Again,' 'Thum-
  belina Mix'
Partners Gypsophila, lobelia, phlox

Below: *Zinnia flowers range in size from tiny buttons to large, decorative bursts of color.*

Appendix I

COMMON & BOTANICAL NAME CHARTS

© Daniel J. Rutkowski, 1990.

Common—Botanical

Common Name	Botanical Name

A

Ageratum	*Ageratum houstonianum*
Alpine Strawberry	*Fragaria vesca americana*
Annual Phlox	*Phlox drummondii 'Blue Beauty'*

Annual Phlox	*Phlox d. 'Dwarf Beauty Mix'*
Annual Phlox	*Phlox d. 'Petticoat'*
Annual Phlox	*Phlox d. 'Salmon Beauty'*
Annual Phlox	*Phlox d. 'Hybrid'*
Arctotis; African Daisy	*Arctotis stoechadifolia*

B

Black-eyed Susan	*Rudbeckia hirta*
Black-eyed Susan Vine	*Thunbergia alata*

Bloodleaf	*Iresine herbstii*
Blue Daisy	*Felicia amelloides*
Blue Daisy	*Felicia a. 'White Felicia'*
Blue Lace Flower; Throatwort	*Trachelium caeruleum*
Browallia	*Browallia speciosa 'Marine Bells'*
Browallia	*Browallia s. 'Silver Bells'*
Bush Violet	*Browallia speciosa*

African daisy plants (left) *are smothered in pert flowers of white or violet. Annual Phlox* (below) .

| Butterfly Flower | *Schizanthus pinnatus 'Hit Parade'* |
| Butterfly Flower | *Schizanthus p. 'Angel Wings'* |

C

| Calendula | *Calendula officinalis* |
| Calendula | *Calendula o. 'Fiesta Mix'* |

Below: *Butterfly flower is also known as Poor Man's orchid because the blooms resemble tiny orchids.*

Calendula	*Calendula o. 'Fiesta Yellow'*
California Poppy	*Eschscholzia californica*
Chamomile	*Matricaria eximia*
Canterbury Bells	*Campanula medium*
Cape Marigold	*Dimorphotheca aurantiaca*
China Aster	*Callistephus chinensis*
China Pink	*Dianthus chinensis*
Chinese Forget-me-not	*Cynoglossum amabile*
Cigar Plant	*Cuphea ignea*
Cineraria	*Senecio* x *hybridus*
Cinquefoil	*Potentilla aurea*
Coleus	*Coleus blumei*
Common Stock	*Matthiola incana 'Brompton Mix'*
Common Stock	*Matthiola i. 'Excelsior Red'*
Common Stock	*Matthiola i. 'Rose Midget'*
Common Sunflower	*Helianthus annuus*
Black-eyed Susan	*Rudbeckia hirta*
Cornflower	*Centaurea cyanus*
Creeping Zinnia	*Sanvitalia procumbens 'Goldbird'*
Cupflower	*Nierembergia hippomanica violacea*
	'Purple Robe'

D

Dahlberg Daisy	*Dyssodia tenuiloba*
Dill-leaf Ursinia	*Ursinia anthemoides*
Dogtooth Violet	*Erythronium dens canis*
Dusty Miller	*Centaurea cineraria*

Masses of white petunias (below) *provide a striking contrast against red geraniums. Opposite:* Pots of petunias and geraniums add interest and accent to the flower bed behind them.

E

English Daisy	*Bellis perennis*
Evening Primrose	*Gaura lindheimeri*

F

Farewell-to-spring	*Godetia amoena; Clarkia amoena*
Feather Cockscomb	*Celosia plumosa 'New Look'*
Feather Cockscomb	*Celosia p. 'Apricot Brandy'*
Flossflower	*Ageratum Houstonianum*
Flowering Tobacco	*Nicotiana alata 'Niki-Pink'*
Flowering Tobacco	*Nicotiana a. 'Niki-Red'*

Flowering Tobacco	*Nicotiana a. 'White Domino'*
Forget-me-not	*Myosotis sylvatica 'Blue Bird'*
Forget-me-not; Alkanet	*Anchusa capensis*
Four-o'clock Flower	*Mirabilis jalapa (red)*
Four-o'clock Flower	*Mirabilis jalapa (yellow)*

G

Garden Verbena	*Verbena hortensis 'Polaris'*
Globe Amaranth	*Gomphrena globosa*
Golden Coreopsis	*Coreopsis tinctoria*

H

Heliotrope	*Heliotropium arborescens*
Heliotrope	*Heliotrope a. 'Black Prince'*
Hollyhock	*Althea rosea*
Hollyhock	*Althea r. 'Majorette Hybrid'*

I

Ice Plant; Livingston Daisy	*Dorotheanthus bellidiflorus*
Ice Plant	*Mesembryanthemum crystallium (red)*
Ice Plant	*Mesembryanthemum crystallium*
Iceland Poppy	*Papaver nudicaule*
Ivy Geranium	*Pelargonium peltatum*

J

Joseph's Coat; Love-lies-bleeding	*Amaranthus tricolor*

K

Knotweed	*Polygonum capitatum*

L

Larkspur	*Consolida ambigua*
Love-in-a-mist	*Nigella damascena 'Miss Jekyll'*

Far left: *The single flowers of the Iceland poppy glisten in shades of yellow as well as orange, red, pink, or white. Near left: The blooms of the Iceland poppy have a texture similar to crepe paper. Below: The graceful flowers of the Iceland poppy are a delight to watch as they shimmer in the breeze.*

M

Marigold	*Tagetes 'Baby Boy'*
Marigold	*Tagetes 'Bonanza Yellow'*
Marigold	*Tagetes 'Dainty Marietta'*
Marigold	*Tagetes 'Disco'*
Marigold	*Tagetes 'Gold Boy'*

Massed flowers of triploid marigolds
(below) *beat the heat throughout the summer.*

Marigold	*Tagetes 'Golden Gem'*
Marigold	*Tagetes 'Lemon Gem'*
Marigold	*Tagetes 'Nugget'*
Marigold	*Tagetes 'Paprika'*
Marigold	*Tagetes 'Queen Sophia'*
Marigold	*Tagetes 'Scarlet Sophie'*

Below: *Like all marigolds, the blooms of triploid marigolds may be yellow, gold, orange, or mahogany.*

Monarch-of-the-Veldt	*Venidium fastuosum*
Monkeyflower	*Mimulus guttatus 'Malibu Yellow'*
Monkeyflower	*Mimulus g. 'Malibu Orange'*
Morning Glory	*Ipomoea purpurea 'Early Call'*
Morning Glory	*Ipomoea p. 'Heavenly Blue'*

N

Nasturtium	*Tropaeolum majus*

P

Painted Tongue	*Salpiglossis sinuata*
Painted Tongue	*Salpiglossis s. 'Splash'*

Passionflower	*Passiflora caerulea*
Pepper Plant	*Capsicum annuum*
Pimpernel	*Anagallis linifolia*

Pincushion Flower	*Scabiosa atro purpurea*
Pocketbook Plant	*Calceolaria herbeohybrida*
Pocketbook Plant	*Calceolaria integrifolia*
Polyanthus Primrose	*Primula x polyantha*
Pot Primrose	*Primula x obconica*
Prairie Gentian	*Lisanthus grandiflorum*

The delicate yet showy flowers of salpiglossis (far left) are effective in beds and borders. The flowers, leaves, flower buds and seeds of nasturtium (near left) can all be used as a peppery addition to salads. Below: Morning glories smother fences, trellises, and walls with their cheerful flowers.

R

Rockrose	*Cistus purpureus*
Rose Moss	*Portulaca grandiflora*

S

Blue Sage	*Salvia farinacea 'Wrightii'*
Sage	*Salvia farinacea 'Victoria'*
Scarlet Sage	*Salvia 'Splendens'*
Shirley Poppy; Corn Poppy	*Papaver rheos*
Snapdragon	*Antirrhinum majus 'Little Darling'*
Snapdragon	*Antirrhinum m. 'Red Flower Carpet'*
Snapdragon	*Antirrhinum m. 'Rocket Mix'*
Snapdragon	*Antirrhinum m. 'Trumpet Serenade'*
Spiderflower	*Cleome hasslerana*
Statice; Sea Lavendar	*Limonium sinuatum*
Strawflower; Everlasting	*Helichrysum bracteatum*
Strawflower	*Helichrysum b. 'Hybrid'*
Strawflower	*Helichrysum b. 'Diamond Head'*
Strawflower	*Helichrysum b. 'Moe's Gold'*
Swan River Daisy	*Brachycome iberidifolia*
Sweet Alyssum	*Lobularia maritima*
Sweet Basil	*Ocimum basilicum*
Sweet Pea	*Lathyrus odoratus*

T

Transvaal Daisy	*Gerbera jamesonii*
Twinspur	*Diascia barberae*
Twinspur	*Diascia b. igescens 'Ruby Fields'*

Top: *White sweet alyssum edges a mixed planting of ageratum, marigolds, black-eyed Susans, and petunias.* Bottom: *The bright red flowers of scarlet sage stand out against dusty miller, ageratum, and sweet alyssum.*

W

Wallflower	*Cheiranthus cheiri*
Wax Begonia	*Begonia semperflorens*
Wax Begonia	*Begonia s. 'Indian Bridge'*
Wax Begonia	*Begonia s. 'Linda'*

Multi-colored zinnias (below) *are as effective in massed plantings as they are as cut flowers.*

Below: *Zinnias reach above marigolds and cornflowers to lead you to the footbridge.*

| Wax Begonia | *Begonia s. 'Vodka'* |
| Wishbone Flower | *Torenia fournieri* |

Z

| Zinnia | *Zinnia elegans 'Dasher Mix'* |

Botanical–Common

Botanical Name	**Common Name**
A	
Ageratum houstonianum	Ageratum; Flossflower
Althea rosea	Hollyhock
Althea r. 'Majorette Hybrid'	Hollyhock
Amaranthus tricolor	Joseph's coat; Love-lies-bleeding
Anagallis linifolia	Pimpernel
Anchusa capensis	Forget-me-not; Alkanet

Antirrhinum majus	Snapdragon
Antirrhinum m. 'Little Darling'	Snapdragon
Antirrhinum m. 'Red Flower Carpet'	Snapdragon

Near left: *Showy spikes of snapdragons bloom in mixed colors and are edged with coleus and white scarlet sage.* Far left: *Tall varieties of snapdragons can be enjoyed in the garden or cut and brought indoors. Neat, tidy mounds of wax begonias* (below) *offer white, pink, or red flowers all summer.*

Antirrhinum m. 'Rocket Mix'	Snapdragon
Antirrhinum m. 'Trumpet Serenade'	Snapdragon
Arctotis stoechadifolia	Arctotis; African Daisy

B

Begonia semperflorens	Wax Begonia
Begonia s. 'Delia'	Wax Begonia
Begonia s. 'Indian bridge'	Wax Begonia
Begonia s. 'Linda'	Wax Begoia
Begonia s. 'Vodka'	Wax Begonia

Below: *Wax begonias make a striking color display in a formal bed.*

Bellis perennis	English Daisy
Brachycome iberidifolia	Swan River Daisy
Browallia speciosa	Browallia; Bush Violet
Browallia s. 'Marine Bells'	Browallia
Browallia s. 'Silver Bells'	Browallia

A narrow bed of wax begonias provides summer-long, low-maintenance color (below).

C

Calceolaria herbeohybrida	Pocketbook Plant
Calceolaria integrifolia	Pocketbook Plant
Calendula officinalis	Calendula
Calendula o. 'Fiesta Mix'	Calendula

Calendula o. 'Fiesta Yellow'	Calendula
Callistephus chinensis	China Aster
Campanula medium	Canterbury Bells
Capsicum annuum	Pepper Plant
Celosia plumosa	Feather Cockscomb
Celosia p. 'New Look'	Feather Cockscomb
Celosia p. 'Apricot Brandy'	Feather Cockscomb
Centaurea cyanus	Cornflower

Opposite: *The petals of calendula are crisp and colorful, in shades of yellow, orange, cream, or apricot.* Below: *The tall, stately stems of rocket larkspur are covered with beautiful blue or white flowers.*

Cheiranthus cheiri	Wallflower
Cleome hasslerana	Spiderflower
Coleus blumei	Coleus
Consolida ambigua	Larkspur

*Cosmos blends with other flowers in a small-space garden (below). Opposite:
The light and airy blooms of cosmos are a delicate foreground to a mixed planting.*

Coreopsis tinctoria	Golden Coreopsis
Correa pulchella	none
Cosmos bipinnatus	Cosmos
Cosmos b. Red Sensation'	Cosmos

Cosmos b. 'Sensation'	Cosmos
Cosmos b. 'Sunny Gold'	Cosmos
Cuphea ignea	Cigar Plant
Cynoglossum amabile	Chinese Forget-me-not

D

Dahlia hybrid	Dahlia
Dahlia 'Bambino Mix'	Dahlia
Dahlia 'Banquet Hybrid'	Dahlia
Dahlia 'Coltness Mix'	Dahlia
Dahlia 'Pom-Pom'	Dahlia
Dianthus chinensis	China Pink
Dianthus c. 'Crimson Charm'	China Pink
Diascia barberae	Twinspur
Diascia r. 'Ruby Fields'	Twinspur
Dimorphotheca aurantiaca	Cape Marigold
Dorotheanthus bellidiflorus	Ice Plant; Livingstone Daisy
Dyssodia tenuiloba	Dahlberg Daisy

E

Eschscholzia californica	California Poppy

F

Felicia amelloides	Blue Daisy
Felicia a. 'White Felicia'	Blue Daisy
Felicia bergerana	Kingfish Daisy
Fragaria vesca	Alpine Strawberry

G

Gaillardia pulchella	Blanketflower
Gazania ringens	none

Gazania r. 'Aztec Orange'	none
Gazania r. 'Aztec Queen'	none
Gazania r. 'Copper King'	none
Gazania r. 'Silver Burgundy'	none
Gerbera jamesonii	Transvaal Daisy
Gerbera j. 'Happipot'	Transvaal Daisy
Godetia (Clarkia) amoena	Farewell-to-spring
Gomphrena globosa	Globe Amaranth

*Bright red Annual phlox harmonize
with blue and lavender petunias* (below).

Below: *As brilliant as its namesake, sunflower fills the garden with golden yellow daisies. Opposite: Sunflowers are easy to grow, good for cutting, and attractive to birds.*

H

Helianthus annuus	Common Sunflower
Helianthus a. 'Sunburst'	Common Sunflower
Helianthus a. 'Sunrose'	Common Sunflower
Helichrysum bracteatum	Strawflower
Helichrysum b. hybrid	Strawflower

Helichrysum b. 'Diamond Head'	Strawflower
Helichrysum b. 'Moe's Gold'	Strawflower
Heliotropium arborescens	Heliotrope
Heliotrope a. 'Black Prince'	Heliotrope

I

New Guinea impatiens and evening primrose edge a mixed flower border (opposite).
Below: *Pink impatiens wrap around the bright red leaves of coleus.*

Bright orange 'Blitz' impatiens (below) is one of the largest-flowered of this annual.
Opposite: The brightly mixed colors of impatiens liven up a shaded section of the garden.

Impatiens 'Mixed Hybrids'	Impatiens
Impatiens wallerana	Impatiens
Ipomoea purpurea	Morning Glory
Ipomoea p. 'Early Call'	Morning Glory
Ipomoea p. 'Heavenly Blue'	Morning Glory
Iresine herbstii	Bloodleaf

L

Lantana camara	Yellow Sage
Lathyrus odoratus	Sweet Pea
Limonium sinuatum	Sea Lavender; Statice
Lisanthus (Eustoma) grandiflorum (white)	Prairie Gentian
Lisanthus (Eustoma) grandiflorum (blue)	Prairie Gentian
Lobelia erinus	Lobelia
Lobelia e. 'Blue Cascade'	Lobelia
Lobelia e. 'Blue Moon'	Lobelia
Lobelia e. 'Cambridge Blue'	Lobelia
Lobelia e. 'Crystal Palace'	Lobelia
Lobelia e. 'Dark cobalt'	Lobelia
Lobularia maritima	Sweet Alyssum
Lobularia m. 'Color Carpet Mix'	Sweet Alyssum
Lobularia m. 'Rosie O' Day'	Sweet Alyssum

M

Matricaria recutita	Chamomile
Matthiola incana	Common Stock
Matthiola i. 'Brompton Mix'	Common Stock
Matthiola i. 'Excelsior Red'	Common Stock
Matthiola i. 'Rose Midget'	Common Stock
Mauryanda erubescens	none
Mesembryanthemum crystallinum (red)	Ice Plant

Mesembryanthemum crystallinum	Ice Plant
Mimulus guttatus	Monkeyflower
Mimulus g. 'Malibu Orange'	Monkeyflower
Mimulus g. 'Malibu Yellow'	Monkeyflower
Mirabilis jalapa (red)	Four-o'clock
Mirabilis jalapa (yellow)	Four-o'clock
Myosotis sylvatica 'Blue Bird'	Forget-me-not

N

Nemesia strumosa 'Rainbow'	none
Nicotiana alata	Flowering Tobacco
Nicotiana a. 'Domino'	Flowering Tobacco
Nicotiana a. 'Niki-pink'	Flowering Tobacco
Nicotiana a. 'Niki-red'	Flowering Tobacco

Below: *Sweet peas cover a fence with cheerful flowers and a delicious fragrance.*

Nierembergia hippomanica violacea	Cupflower
Nierembergia v. 'Purple Robe'	Cupflower
Nigella damascena	Love-in-a-mist
Nigella d. 'Miss Jekyll'	Love-in-a-mist
Nolana paradoxa	none

Pink and white petunias (below left) *make a striking effect in a sunny border. The solid-colored, starred, or streaked flowers of petunias* (below right) *bloom in every color of the rainbow.*

Nolana paradoxa	none

O

Ocimum basilicum	Sweet Basil
Osteopermum (ecklonis)	African Daisy

P

Papaver nudicaule	Iceland Poppy
Papaver rheos	Shirley Poppy; Corn Poppy
Pelargonium peltatum	Ivy Geranium
Pelargonium x *hortorum*	Zonal Geranium
Pelargonium x *domesticum*	Geranium

Petunia hybrida	Petunia
Petunia 'Blue Flash'	Petunia
Petunia 'Flare'	Petunia
Petunia 'Rare Madness'	Petunia
Petunia 'Red Cascade'	Petunia

Below: *Petunias are equally dramatic in formal beds, shown here.*

Petunia 'Summer Madness'	Petunia
Petunia 'Super Cascade'	Petunia
Phlox drummondii	Annual Phlox
Phlox d. 'Blue Beauty'	Annual Phlox
Phlox d. 'Dwarf Beauty Mix'	Annual Phlox
Phlox d. 'Hybrid'	Annual Phlox
Phlox d. 'Petticoat'	Annual Phlox
Phlox d. 'Salmon Beauty'	Annual Phlox
Polygonum capitatum	Knotweed
Portulaca grandiflora	Rose Moss
Portulaca g. 'Magic Carpet'	Rose Moss
Portulaca g. 'Sunnyside Coral'	Rose Moss
Potentilla aurea	Cinquefoil

Red scarlet sage is a striking complement to the blue flowers of Salvia farinacea (below).

Potentilla a. 'Goldrop'	Cinquefoil
Primula x *obconica*	Primrose; Primula
Primula x *polyantha*	Primrose

R

Rudbeckia hirta	Black-eyed Susan
Rudbeckia h. 'Marmalade'	Black-eyed Susan

S

Salpiglossis sinuata	Painted Tongue
Salpiglossis s. 'Bolero'	Painted Tongue
Salpiglossis s. 'Splash'	Painted Tongue
Salvia farinacea	Cup Sage
Salvia f. 'Argent White'	Sage
Salvia f. 'Victoria'	Cup Sage
Salvia f. 'Wrightii'	Sage
Salvia 'Splendens'	Scarlet Sage
Salvia s. 'Flamenco'	Scarlet Sage
Sanvitalia procumbens	Creeping Zinnia
Sanvitalia p. 'Goldbird'	Creeping Zinnia
Scabiosa atro purpurea	Pincushion Flower
Schizanthus pinnatus	Poor Man's Orchid
Schizanthus p. 'Angel Wings'	Butterfly Flower
Schizanthus p. 'Hit Parade'	Butterfly Flower
Senecio x *hybridus*	Cineraria
Senecio maritima	Dusty Miller

T

Tagetes erecta	Marigold
Tagetes 'Baby Boy'	Marigold
Tagetes 'Bonanza Yellow'	Marigold
Tagetes 'Dainty Marietta'	Marigold
Tagetes 'Disco'	Marigold
Tagetes 'Gold Boy'	Marigold
Tagetes 'Golden Gem'	Marigold
Tagetes 'Lemon Gold'	Marigold
Tagetes 'Nugget'	Marigold
Tagetes 'Paprika'	Marigold
Tagetes 'Queen Sophia'	Marigold
Tagetes 'Scarlet Sophie'	Marigold
Thunbergia alata	Black-eyed Susan Vine
Tithonia rotundifolia	Mexican Sunflower
Torenia fournieri	Wishbone Flower
Trachelium caeruleum	Blue Lace Flower; Throatwort
Tropaeolum majus	Nasturtium

U

Ursinia anthemoides	Dill-leaf Ursinia

V

Venidium fastuosum	Monarch-of-the-veldt; Cape Daisy
Verbena x *hybrida*	Garden Verbena
Verbena h. 'Polaris'	Garden Verbena
Verbena h. 'Romantic Burgundy'	Garden Verbena
Verbena h. 'St. Paul'	Garden Verbena

Verbena h. 'Springtime'	Garden Verbena
Viola tricolor	Johnny-jump-up
Viola t. 'Bambino Mix'	Violet
Viola t. 'Ruby Queen'	Violet
Viola wittrockiana	Pansy
Viola w. 'Red Wing'	Pansy

Z

Zinnia angustifolia	Creeping Zinnia
Zinnia a. 'Classic'	Zinnia
Zinnia elegans	Zinnia
Zinnia e. 'Dasher Mix'	Zinnia
Zinnia e. 'Cut n' Come Again'	Zinnia
Zinnia e. 'Thumbelina Mix'	Zinnia

Below: *Brightly colored zinnia flowers blend well with other annuals in a mixed border.*

Appendix II

BEST ANNUALS FOR SPECIFIC CONDITIONS

© Daniel J. Rutkowski, 1990.

Top left: *Mounds of 'Heavenly Blue' morning glories open with the sunrise to add charm to the garden.* Bottom left: *Rose moss thrives where it's hot and dry and the soil is sandy, its flowers opening with the sunrise. The vivid blooms of scarlet sage* (opposite) *are a true eye-catcher.*

Dry Soil Conditions

Arctotis stoechadifolia grandis (African Daisy)

Centaurea cyanus (Bachelor's Button, Cornflower)

Convolvulus tricolor (Dwarf Morning Glory)

Coreopsis tinctoria (Calliopsis)

Delphinium ajacia (Larkspur)

Dimorphotheca (various) (Cape Marigold)

Eschscholzia californica (California Poppy)

Euphorbia marginata (Snow-on-the-mountain)

Gaillardia pulchella (Rose-ring Gaillardia)

Gypsophila elegans (Baby's Breath)

Helianthus annuus (Sunflower)

Ipomoea purpurea (Morning Glory)

Mirabilis jalapa (Four-o'clock)

Phlox drummondii (Annual Phlox)

Portulaca grandiflora (Rose Moss)

Salvia splendens (Scarlet Sage)

Zinnia elegans (Giant-flowered Zinnia)

Soil Between Paved Areas

For Edging
Ageratum (various)
Antirrhinum (dwarf kinds)
(Snapdragon)
Begonia semperflorens (Wax Begonia)
Brachycome iberidifolia (Swan River
Daisy)
Browallia americana (Browallia)
Calendula officinalis (Calendula,
Marigold)
Celosia (various) (Cockscomb)
Centaurea cineraria (Dusty Miller)
Coreopsis tinctoria (Calliopsis)
Dianthus chinensis (China Pink)
Eschscholzia californica (California
Poppy)
Iberis umbellata (Globe Candytuft)
Linum grandiflorum 'Rubrum' (Scarlet
Flax)
Lobelia erinus (Lobelia)
Petunia (various) (Petunia)
Phlox drummondii (Annual Phlox)
Portulaca grandiflora (Rose Moss)
Tagetes patula (Marigold)
Tropaeolum majus (Nasturtium)
Verbena (various)

Opposite: *Low-growing French marigolds add sunny color to a border.* Top right: *Impatiens bordered in lobelia clearly mark the way down the garden path.* Bottom right: *The clustered flowers of candytuft may be pink, crimson, rose, lavender, or white.*

City Conditions

Ageratum (various)
Antirrhinum (Snapdragon)
Cleome (Spiderflower)
Lobelia erinus (Lobelia)
Lobularia (Sweet Alyssum)
Mirabilis (Four-o'clock)
Nicotiana (Flowering Tobacco)
Petunia
Phlox (Phlox)
Salvia (Sage)
Tagetes (Marigold)
Verbena
Zinnia

Far left: *Airy spider flowers in the background contrast with the bolder, golden-colored marigolds in the foreground.* Near left: *'Peter Pan' is a dwarf zinnia, useful for small gardens, edgings, and borders.*

Shady Places

Ageratum houstonianum (Flossflower)
Bellis perennis (English Daisy)
Catharanthus roseus (Vinca Rosea)
Madagascar Periwinkle
Centaurea americana (Basketflower)
Centaurea moschata (Sweet Sultan)
Clarkia elegans (Clarkia)
Delphinium ajacis (Larkspur)
Gerbera jamesonii (Transvaal Daisy)
Godetia amoena (Farewell-to-spring)
Impatiens balsamina (Balsam)
Lobelia erinus (Lobelia)
Lobularia maritima (Sweet Alyssum)
Lupinus hartwegii (Lupine, annual)
Myosotis sylvatica (Forget-me-not)
Nicotiana alata (Flowering Tobacco)
Phlox drummondii (Annual Phlox)
Primula malacoides (Fairy Primrose)
Salpiglossis sinuata (Painted Tongue)
Viola tricolor hortensis (Pansy)

Cut Flowers

Amaranthus caudatus
(Love-lies-bleeding)
Antirrhinum majus (Snapdragon)
Arctotis stoechadifolia grandis (African
Daisy)
Calendula officinalis (Calendula, Pot
Marigold)
Callistephus chinensis (Aster, China
Aster)
Centaurea moschata (Sweet Sultan)
Chrysanthemum
Clarkia elegans (Clarkia)
Cosmos
Delphinium ajacis (Larkspur)
Dianthus chinensis (China Pink)
Dimorphoteca (various) (African
Daisy, Cape Marigold)
Eschscholzia californica

(California Poppy)
Gaillardia
Gomphrena globosa (Globe Amaranth)
Gypsophila (Baby's Breath)
Helianthus annuus (Sunflower)
Helichrysum bractaetum (Strawflower)
Lathyrus odoratus (Sweet Pea)
Matthiola incana (Stock)
Nigella damescena (Love-in-a-mist)
Papaver glaucum (Tulip Poppy)
Phlox drummondii (Annual Phlox)
Salpiglossis sinuata (Painted Tongue)
Scabiosa atro purpurea (Pinchusion
Flower)
Senecio elegans (Purple Ragwort)
Tagetes (Marigold)
Verbena hybrida (Hortensis)
Zinnia elegans (Small-flowered Zinnia)

The crested blooms of 'Bonanza' French marigold (far left) are pretty in flower arrangements. China aster (near left) fills the garden with blooms from midsummer until fall. Below: The black centers of sunflower are striking against the golden petals in the garden or in a vase.

Left: *Red verbena mixes well with pink solid-colored and starred petunias and purple and white lobelia.* Above: *Snapdragons can fill a garden or a room in the house with a light, spicy fragrance.* Above right: *'Plum pudding' petunias.*

Fragrance

Antirrhinum majus
(Snapdragon)

Calendula officinalis (Calendula,
Pot Marigold)

Delphinium ajacis (Larkspur)

Iberis umbellata (Globe Candytuft)

Lathyrus odoratus (Sweet Pea)

Lobularia maritima (Sweet Alyssum)

Lupinus luteus (Yellow Lupine)

Matthiola bicornis (Night-scented
Stock)

Matthiola incana (Stock)

Nicotiana sanderae (Flowering
Tobacco)

Oenothera biennis (Evening Primrose)

Petunia

Phlox drummondii (Annual Phlox)

Scabiosa atro purpurea (Pincushion
Flower)

Tagetes (Marigold)

Tropaeolum majus (Nasturtium)

Appendix III

ANNUALS BY COLOR

© Daniel J. Rutkowski, 1990.

WHITE

Ageratum houstonianum (Flossflower)

Antirrhinum majus (Snapdragon)

Arctotis stoechadifolia grandis (African Daisy)

Begonia semperflorens (Wax Begonia)

Brachycome iberidifolia (Swan River Daisy)

Browallia americana (Browallia)

Calendula officinalis (Calendula, Pot Marigold)

Callistephus chinensis (Aster or China Aster)

Campanula medium (Canterbury Bells)

Catharanthus roseus (Vinca rosea) (Madagascar Periwinkle)

Centaurea cyanus (Bachelor's Button, Cornflower)

Centaurea imperialis (Royal Sweet Sultan)

Chrysanthemum

Clarkia amoena (Farewell-to-spring)

Clarkia elegans (Clarkia)

Clarkia unguiculata (Mountain Garland)

Cleome hasslerana (Spiderflower)

Cosmos bipinnatus (Cosmos)

Delphinium ajacis (Larkspur)

Dianthus chinensis (China Pinks)

Dimorphotheca sinuata (Cape Marigold, African Daisy)

Euphorbia marginata (Snow-on-the-mountain)

Gomphrena globosa (Globe Amaranth)

Gypsophila elegans (Baby's Breath)

Helichrysum bracteatum (Strawflower)

Iberis amara (Rocket Candytuft)

Iberis umbellata (Globe Candytuft)

Impatiens balsamina (Balsam)

Ipomea purpurea (Morning Glory)

Lathyrus odoratus (Sweet Pea)

Limonium Sinuatum (Statice, Sea Lavender)

Lobelia erinus (Lobelia)

Lobularia maritima (Sweet Alyssum)

Lupinus mutablis (Lupine)

Matthiola incana (Stock)

Mirabilis jalapa (Four-o'clock)

Nemesia strumosa (Nemesia)

Nicotiana alata (Flowering Tobacco)

Nicotiana sylvestris

Nigella damascena (Love-in-a-mist)

Oenothera biennis (Evening Primrose)

Papaver nudicaule (Iceland Poppy)

Papaver rheos (Shirley Poppy)

Petunia hybrids

Phlox drummondii (Annual Phlox)

Physalis alkekengi (Chinese Lantern)

Portulaca grandiflora (Rose Moss)

Sweet Pea, Lathyrus odoratus, *in garden setting* (below).

Scabiosa atro purpurea
(Pincushion Flower)

Schizanthus pinnatus
(Butterfly Flower)

Senecia elegans (Purple
Ragwort)

Tropaeolum majus
(Nasturtium)

Verbena hybrida
(hortensis) (Garden
Verbena)

Viola tricolor hortensis
(Pansy)

Zinnia angustifolia
(Mexican Zinnia)

Zinnia elegans
(Small-flowered
Zinnia)

Zinnia elegans
(Giant-flowered
Zinnia)

Top: *Small, fuzzy blooms of ageratum grow through a ground cover to give it color.* Bottom: *Cupflowers are effective in beds, borders, edgings, and rock gardens.*

BLUE

Ageratum houstonianum (Flossflower)

Callistephus chinensis (Aster, China Aster)

Campanula medium (Canterbury Bells)

Centaurea cyanus (Bachelor's Button, Cornflower)

Convolvulus tricolor (Dwarf Morning Glory)

Cosmos

Delphinium ajacis (Larkspur)

Ipomoea purpurea (Morning Glory)

Limonium sinuatum (Statice, Sea Lavender)

Linaria maroccana (Baby Snapdragon)

Lobelia erinus (Lobelia)

Matthiola incana (Stock)

Myosotis sylvatica (Forget-me-not)

Nemesia strumosa (Nemesia)

Nierembergia caerulea (Blue Cupflower)

Nigella damascena (Love-in-a-mist)

Papaver rheos (Shirley Poppy)

Salvia (Sage)

Scabiosa atro purpurea (Pincushion Flower)

Trachymene caerulea (Blue Lace Flower)

Verbena hybrids

Viola tricolor hortensis (Pansy)

Zinnia elegans (Giant-flowered Zinnia)

LAVENDER

Callistephus chinensis
(Aster, China Aster)

Centaurea cyanus
(Bachelor's Button,
Cornflower)

Clarkia elegans
(Clarkia)

Delphinium ajacis
(Larkspur)

Limonium sinuatum
(Statice, Sea
Lavender)

Lobularia maritima
(Sweet Alyssum)

Zinnia elegans
(Small-flowered
Zinnia)

LILAC

Browallia speciosa
major (Browallia)

Cosmos

Iberis umbellata (Globe
Candytuft)

Lathyrus odoratus
(Sweet Pea)

Lupinus (Lupine)

Matthiola bicornus
(Night-scented
Stock)

Petunia hybrids

Phlox drummondii
(Annual Phlox)

PURPLE

Antirrhinum majus
(Snapdragon)

Browallia americana
(Browallia)

Browallia speciosa
major

Dianthus chinensis
(China Pink)

Impatiens

Ipomoea purpurea
(Morning Glory)

Lathyrus odoratus
(Sweet Pea)

Linaria maroccana
(Baby Snapdragon)

Lobularia maritima
(Sweet Alyssum)

Lupinus (Lupine)

Matthiola bicornus
(Night-scented
Stock)

Matthiola incana
(Stock)

Nemesia strumosa
(Nemesia)

Petunia hybrids

Phlox drummondii
(Annual Phlox)

Salpiglossis sinuata
(Painted Tongue)

Scabiosa atropurpurea
(Pincushion Flower)

Schizanthus pinnatus
(Butterfly Flower)

Senecio elegans (Purple
Ragwort)

Verbena hybrids

Viola tricolor hortensis
(Pansy)

Zinnia elegans
(Giant-flowered
Zinnia)

Below: *There are few truer-blue flowers than the flowers of the morning glory.*

VIOLET

Antirrhinum majus (Snapdragon)	Ipomoea purpurea (Morning Glory)	Trachymene caerulea (Blue Lace Flower)
Gomphrena globosa (Globe Amaranth)	Lobelia erinus (Lobelia)	Zinnia elegans (Giant-flowered Zinnia)

RED

Antirrhinum majus
(Snapdragon)

Brachycome
iberidifolia (Swan
River Daisy)

Callistephus chinensis
(Aster, China Aster)

Convolvulus

Helichrysum
bracteatum
(Strawflower)

Impatiens balsamina
(Balsam)

Ipomoea purpurea
(Morning Glory)

Mirabilis jalapa
(Four-o'clock)

Papaver glaucum (Tulip
Poppy)

Primula malocoides
(Fairy Primrose)

Salpiglossis sinuata
(Painted Tongue)

Masses of scarlet sage are attention-getters in the garden (below).

SCARLET

Linum grandiflorum
'Rubrum' (Scarlet
Flax)

Salvia splendens
(Scarlet Sage)

Verbena hybrida
hortensis (Garden
Verbena)

Zinnia elegans
(Small-flowered
Zinnia, Giant-
flowered Zinnia)

CRIMSON

Amaranthus caudatus
(Love-lies-bleeding)

Gomphrena globosa
(Globe Amaranth)

Linaria (Baby
Snapdragon)

Matthiola incana
(Stock)

Nicotiana

Papaver rheos (Shirley
Poppy)

Portulaca grandiflora
(Rose Moss)

Tropaeolum majus
(Nasturtium)

MAGENTA

Impatiens

Wine

Centaurea cyanus
(Bachelor's Button,
Cornflower)

Gaillardia pulchella
(Rose-ring
Gaillardia)

MAUVE

Impatiens

Schizanthus pinnatus
(Butterfly Flower)

MAROON

Coreopsis tinctoria
(Calliopsis)

Gaillardia pulchella
(Rose-ring
Gaillardia)

Tropaeolum majus
(Nasturtium)

Zinnia angustifolia
(Mexican Zinnia)

Carmine

Delphinium ajacis
(Larkspur)

GOLD

Calendula officinalis (Calendula, Pot Marigold)

Celosia 'Plumosa' (Plume Cockscomb)

Eschscholzia californica (California Poppy)

Gomphrena globosa (Globe Amaranth)

Helianthus annuus (Sunflower)

Tagetes (Marigold)

BRONZE

Chrysanthemum

ORANGE

Antirrhinum majus (Snapdragon)

Calendula officinalis (Calendula, Pot Marigold)

Chrysanthemum

Clarkia

Coreopsis tinctoria (Golden Coreopsis)

Eschscholzia californica (California Poppy)

Gerbera jamesonii (Transvaal Daisy)

Nemesia strumosa (Nemesia)

Papaver rheos (Shirley Poppy)

Portulaca grandiflora (Rose Moss)

Salpiglossis sinuata (Painted Tongue)

Tithonia rotundifolia (Mexican Sunflower)

Viola tricolor hortensis (Pansy)

Zinnia angustifolia (Mexican Zinnia)

Zinnia elegans (Small-flowered Zinnia, Giant-flowered Zinnia)

Tagetes (Marigold)

Far left: *'Inca' African marigolds are the primary component in a floral design.*
Near left: *Orange French marigolds glow next to verbena and rose moss. Marigold mix well with almost any other annual in a sunny border (below).*

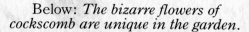

Below: *The bizarre flowers of cockscomb are unique in the garden.*

YELLOW

Antirrhinum majus (Snapdragon)

Calendula officinalis (Calendula, Pot Marigold)

Callistephus chinensis (Aster, China Aster)

Celosia 'Plumosa' (Feather Cockscomb)

Centaurea moschata (Sweet Sultan)

Chrysanthemum

Clarkia

Coreopsis tinctoria (Golden Coreopsis)

Cosmos sulphureus (Yellow Cosmos)

Dimorphoteca sinuata (African Daisy, Cape Marigold)

Eschscholzia californica (California Poppy)

Gaillardia pulchella (Rose-ring Gaillardia)

Gerbera jamesonii (Transvaal Daisy)

Limonium sinuatum (Statice, Sea Lavender)

Linaria (Baby Snapdragon)

Lupinus mutabilis (Lupine)

Lupinus luteus (Yellow Lupine)

Matthiola incana (Stock)

Mirabalis jalapa (Four-o'clock)

Nemesia strumosa (Nemesia)

Oenothera biennis (Evening Primrose)

Portulaca grandiflora (Rose Moss)

Salpiglossis sinuata (Painted Tongue)

Tagetes (Marigold)

Thunbergia alata (Clockvine)

ROSE

Begonia semperflorens
(Wax Begonia)

Centaurea moschata
(Sweet Sultan)

Clarkia amoena
(Farewell-to-spring)

Clarkia elegans
(Clarkia)

Cosmos bipinnatus
(Cosmos)

Delphinium ajacis
(Larkspur)

Dianthus barbatus
(Sweet William)

Eschscholzia
californica
(California Poppy)

Gyposophila elegans
(Baby's Breath)

Iberis umbellata (Globe
Candytuft)

Impatiens balsamina
(Balsam)

Lathyrus odoratus
(Sweet Pea)

Limonium sinuatum
(Statice, Sea
Lavender)

Linum grandiflorum
'Rubrum' (Scarlet
Flax)

Lobularia maritima
(Sweet Alyssum)

Matthiola incana
(Stock)

Nemesia strumosa
(Nemesia)

Nigella damascena
(Love-in-a-mist)

Oenothera biennis
(Evening Primrose)

Petunia hybrids

Phlox drummondii
(Annual Phlox)

Polygonum orientale
(Princess Feather)

Primula malacoides
(Fairy Primrose)

Salvia splendens
(Scarlet Sage)

Scabiosa atropurpurea
(Pincushion Flower)

Schizanthus pinnatus
(Butterfly Flower)

Senecio elegans
(Purpose Ragwort)

Viola tricolor hortensis
(Pansy)

*The cheerful trumpets of
petunias (below) enliven a garden wall.*

*In the pink, this mixed border contains spider
flower, New Guinea impatiens, and wax begonias* (below).

PINK

Ageratum
houstonianum
(Flossflower)

Antirrhinum majus
(Snapdragon)

Begonia semperflorens
(Wax Begonia)

Callistephus chinensis
(China Aster)

Campanula
(Canterbury Bells)

Catharanthus roseus
(Vinca rosea)
(Madagascar
Periwinkle)

Celosia 'Plumosa'
(Cockscomb)

Centaurea cyanus
(Bachelor's Button,
Cornflower)

Clarkia elegans
(Clarkia)

Cleome hasslerana
(Spiderflower)

Cosmos bipannatus
(Cosmos)

Cryophytum
crystallinum (Ice
Plant)

Delphinium ajacia
(Larkspur)

Dianthus chinensis
(China Pink)

Eschscholzia
californica
(California Poppy)

Gypsophila elegans
(Baby's Breath)

Helichrysum
bracteatum
(Strawflower)

Impatiens balsamina
(Balsam)

Ipomoea purpurea
(Morning Glory)

Lathyrus odoratus
(Sweet Pea, Summer)

Lobelia erinus
(Lobelia)

Lupinus hartwegii
(Lupine, annual)

Matthiola incana
(Stock)

Mirabilis jalapa
(Four-o'clock)

Myosotis sylvatica
(Forget-me-not)

Nemesia strumosa
(Nemesia)

Papaver rheos (Shirley
Poppy)

Petunia hybrids

Polygonum orientale
(Princess Feather)

Primula malocoides
(Fairy Primrose)

Salpiglossis sinuata
(Painted Tongue)

Salvia splendens
(Scarlet Sage)

Tropaeolum majus
(Nasturtium)

Verbena hybrida
(hortensis) (Garden
Verbena)

SALMON

Delphinium ajacis
(Larkspur)

Dimorphoteca sinuata
(African Daisy, Cape
Marigold)

Iberis umbellata (Globe
Candytuft)

Papaver rheos (Shirley
Poppy)

Hardiness Zone Map

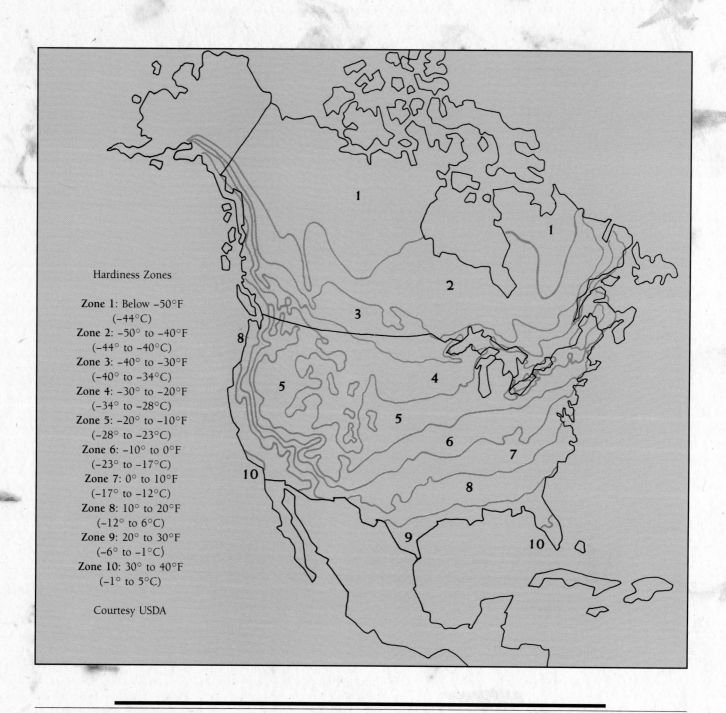

Hardiness Zones

Zone 1: Below –50°F
(–44°C)
Zone 2: –50° to –40°F
(–44° to –40°C)
Zone 3: –40° to –30°F
(–40° to –34°C)
Zone 4: –30° to –20°F
(–34° to –28°C)
Zone 5: –20° to –10°F
(–28° to –23°C)
Zone 6: –10° to 0°F
(–23° to –17°C)
Zone 7: 0° to 10°F
(–17° to –12°C)
Zone 8: 10° to 20°F
(–12° to 6°C)
Zone 9: 20° to 30°F
(–6° to –1°C)
Zone 10: 30° to 40°F
(–1° to 5°C)

Courtesy USDA

Below: *Sweet William catchfly doesn't mind cool springs and blooms with yellow yarrow, a perennial.*

GLOSSARY

ALTERNATE Arranged singly along a shoot

AXIL The angle formed by a leafstalk and the stem

AXIS The central stalk of a compound leaf

BASAL LEAF Leaf at base of a stem

BIENNIAL A plant whose life span extends to two growing seasons

BRACT A modified and often scalelike leaf

BUD An undeveloped leaf or flower

CALYX The sepals of a flower

CLONE A group of plants originating by vegetative propagation from a single plant

COMPOUND LEAF A leaf made up of several leaflets

CORM An underground stem

CORONA A crownlike structure on some corollas, as in daffodils and the Milkweed family

CORYMB A flattened flower cluster

CREEPER A trailing shoot that takes root at the nodes

CROWN Part of a plant, usually at soil level

CULTIVAR A man-made plant variety

CUTTING A piece of plant without roots

CYME A branching flower cluster that blooms from the center toward the edges

DISSECTED A deeply cut leaf

DIVISION Propagation by division of crowns into segments

EVERLASTING Flowers for dried arrangements

FLOWERHEAD A short, tight cluster of flowers

GENUS A group of closely related species; plural, *genera*

GLAUCOUS Covered with a waxy bloom or fine pale powder

HIRSUTE Covered with hairs

HYBRID A plant resulting from a cross between two parent plants belonging to different species

INFLORESCENCE Flower cluster

INVASIVE Spreading

LANCEOLATE Shaped like a spear or lance

LAYERING Propagation in which a stem sends out roots

LEAF AXIL The angle between the petiole of a leaf and the stem

LEAFLET Subdivisions of a compound leaf

LOBE A segment of a petal

MARGIN Edge of a leaf

MIDRIB The mid-vein of a leaf or leaflet

OPPOSITE Arranged along a twig or shoot in pairs, with one on each side

OVATE Egg-shaped

PALMATE Having veins or leaflets arranged like the fingers on a hand, arising from a single point

PANICLE An open flower cluster

PELTATE A leaf to which the stalk is attached under the surface

PERENNIAL A plant whose life span extends over several growing seasons.

PETAL One of a series of flower parts

PETIOLE The stalk of a leaf

PINNATE A leaf with a series of leaflets

PROPAGATE To produce new plants, either by vegetative means or by sowing seeds

PROSTRATE Lying on the ground

RACEME A flower cluster on which individual flowers bloom on small stalks from a larger, central stalk

RHIZOME A horizontal underground stem

ROSETTE A circular cluster of leaves; usually basal

RUNNER A prostrate shoot

SPIKE An unbranched inflorescence with stemless flowers

SUCCULENT A plant with thick, fleshy leaves

TERMINAL Tip of a stem or shoot

TOOTHED Margin shallowly divided into small, toothlike segments

TUFTED Growing in dense clumps

UMBEL A flower cluster

VARIEGATED Marked, striped

WHORL Leaves and petals arranged in a ring

—MAIL-ORDER SUPPLIERS—

The following list of mail-order suppliers is not an endorsement for these suppliers. These are companies I have dealt with and find satisfactory.

A SELECTED LIST OF MAJOR SUPPLIERS FOR SEEDS AND CATALOGS

UNITED STATES

W. Atlee Burpee Company
300 Park Avenue
Warminster, PA 18974

Farmer Seed & Nursery Company
818 N.W. Fourth Street
Box 129
Fairibault, MN 55021

Henry Field Seed & Nursery Company
407 Sycamore Street
Shenandoah, IA 51602

Gurney Seed and Nursery Company
1224 Page Street
Yankton, SD 57078

Joseph Harris Company, Inc.
3670 Buffalo Road
Rochester, NY 14624

Herbst Brothers Seedsmen, Inc.
1000 N. Main Street
Brewster, NY 10509

J.W. Jung Seed Company
335 S. High Street
Randolph, WI 53957

Liberty Seed Company
128 First Drive SE
Box 806
New Philadelphia, OH 44663

Nichols Garden Nursery
1190 N. Pacific Highway
Albany, OR 97321

L.L. Olds Seed Company
Box 7790
2901 Packers Avenue
Madison, WI 53707

George W. Park Seed Company, Inc.
Box 31
Greenwood, SC 29647

R.H. Shumway Seedsman, Inc.
Box 1
Graniteville, SC 29829

Stokes Seeds, Inc.
737 Main Street
Box 548
Buffalo, NY 14240

Thompson & Morgan, Inc.
Box 1308
Jackson, NJ 08527

Otis Twilley Seed Company, Inc.
Box 65
Trevose, PA 19047

W.J. Unwin Ltd.
Box 9
Farmingdale, NJ 07727

CANADA

Dominion Seed House
115 Guelph Street
Georgetown, Ont.
L7G 4A2

Photo Credits

© Andrew Addkison: 54 top, 78 bottom, 88 top.

© Jack Barnich: 59 top, 60 top, 66 bottom, 70 top, 79 bottom, 91 top, 96 bottom.

© Derek Fell: 3, 9, 11, 12, 13 left, 13 right, 15, 16, 17, 18, 20-21, 23, 24, 25 left, 25 right, 26, 28, 29, 30, 33 top, 33 bottom, 35, 36, 37, 39, 40, 41, 43, 45, 46, 47, 49, 51 top, 51 bottom, 52 bottom, 53 top, 53 bottom, 54 bottom, 55, 56 bottom, 57 bottom, 63 bottom, 64 bottom, 67, 68 bottom, 70 top, 71, 73 top, 73 bottom, 74 top, 75 top, 76 top, 77 bottom, 78 top, 82 bottom, 83 bottom, 84 top, 85 top, 85 bottom, 86 bottom, 87 top, 87 bottom, 88 bottom, 89 top, 90 top, 90 bottom, 93 top, 94 top, 96 top, 97 top, 97 bottom, 98 bottom, 99 top, 100 top, 100 bottom, 101 bottom, 105 bottom, 106 top, 106 bottom, 107 top, 109 top, 111 top, 111 bottom, 112 top, 113, 115, 116, 117, 118, 120, 124, 125, 126 left, 127, 130, 131, 132, 132 top, 133, 134, 135, 137, 138, 139, 141, 142, 145, 146, 147, 149, 150 left, 150 right, 151, 152, 155, 157, 158, 158 top, 159, 160, 161, 161 top, 162, 162-163, 165, 166, 167 right, 169, 171, 172 top, 175, 176, 178, 178 top, 179, 180, 181, 182, 185, 186-187, 189, 190.

© Cindy Gilberg: 102 bottom, 103 bottom.

© Deborah Kaplan: 172.

© Jack Kramer: 50 top, 50 bottom, 52 top, 54 top, 56 top, 57 top, 58 top, 58 bottom, 59 top, 59 bottom, 61 top, 61 bottom, 62 bottom, 63 top, 65 bottom, 66 bottom, 68 top, 69 bottom, 70 bottom, 72 top, 72 bottom, 74 bottom, 76 bottom, 77 top, 79 top, 80 top, 80 bottom, 81 bottom, 83 top, 86 top, 91 bottom, 92 top, 92 bottom, 93 bottom, 97 top, 102 top, 104 top, 104 bottom, 105 top,107 bottom, 110 top, 110 bottom, 112 bottom.

© Alan Oddie/PhotoEdit: 143.

© Eda Rogers/PhotoEdit: 62 top, 69 top, 82 top, 95 top, 98 top, 99 bottom, 103 top, 108, 109 bottom, 122 top, 122 bottom, 126 right, 136, 164 left, 164 right, 167 left.

© Ede Rothaus: 75 bottom, 95 bottom.

© Daniel Rutkowski 1990, all rights reserved: 10, 48, 114, 156, 168.

© Anita Sabarese: 129 top, 129 bottom, 144.

© Carol Simowitz: 121.

© George Taloumis: 60 bottom, 63 top, 64 top, 65 top, 66 top, 81 top, 84 bottom, 89 bottom, 101 top.

© Elizabeth Zuckerman/PhotoEdit: 123.